NINE LIVES AND RUNNING

by

Alex Jadah

© *TASTE OF READING PUBLISHERS*

NINE LIVES AND RUNNING
ISBN O - 9698914 - 0 - 7

Copyright ©1996

Published by TASTE OF READING PUBLISHERS
P.O. Box 9001
SYLVAN LAKE, AB.
C a n a d a
T4S 1S6

Front Cover : Polish Farmer's Market 1939 - oil on masonite
by Alex Jadah

Illustrations: line drawings from memory by Alex Jadah -
photographs from friends and archives

Back Cover: Author's photo by Andrew M. Kobos

Book production: Bunker to Bunker Books, Winnipeg, MB, Canada

Printed and bound in Canada by Hignell Printing, Winnipeg, MB.

TABLE OF CONTENTS

This book is dedicated to my wonderful grandchildren and to the grandchildren of all those who were uprooted by World War 2, that they might know a piece of history

INTRODUCTION

Nine Lives and Running - an unusual book in the English language readership realm. Unusual for several reasons:

- One of the very few authentic relations in English on the dark years of suffering, horror, death and relentless struggle of the Polish nation against the German Nazi occupiers in the years 1939-1945.
- The vivid personal, illustrated, retrospective account of these years by a man who, as a teenager, confronted by the loss of his country's independence joined many of those who never gave up, no matter the price - frequently the ultimate one.
- Authentic, yet a literary valuable book with an insight into the Author's mind.

Alex Jada(c)h was one of the unspoken, active participants of this struggle for Poland - an Underground soldier of the undefeated Poland. Surrounded by terror and death, he took part in several of the most daring actions of the Underground Union of the Armed Struggle (ZWZ) and later Home Army (AK). His recollections from those actions conform dependable sources on the history of the Underground.

Caught by the Germans in a "street-catch" ["lapanka"] in the spring of 1944, Alex was sent to Germany and later to the German occupied northern Finland and reduced to a slave-labourer. Thus perhaps, he was spared a heroic death in the Warsaw Uprising of 1944. In the book, he tells about the inhumane conditions in the labor camps which nonetheless were much more human than those in the German concentration death-camps.

Having had a number of close encounters with death which rationally he should not have survived, Alex did prevail. Perhaps someone somewhere had ensured it; if for nothing else then to enable Alex, more than half a century later, to report to the outside world on the horrors of the total war and the strength of the Polish spirit.

A much needed book.

Andrew M. Kobos, PhD
Edmonton, Alberta, 1996

Chapter 1

THE EXCITING PRE-WAR YEARS

"Drop your rifle and raise your hands," the words fell like drops of icy water behind my collar, sharp and stinging.

I thought someone was joking till I saw my two friends lined up against the wall disarmed and standing with their hands up. A young German, younger than we, was pointing a Schmeisser at them. There were two other Germans close to me, almost kids, pointing their submachine guns at me. The Polish speaking soldier smiled.

"So, we've picked you up, you Polish swines, you f.... partisans, one by one. Our superiors told us how ugly you are and how you stink."

A German motorcycle with a side wagon was parked further away. The three of them must have been on patrol and we had not spotted them.

I dropped my Mauser and walked toward my friends. We were lined up against the thick timber of a farm house. The one who spoke Polish searched us. He was young and inexperienced and did not do a very good

job. The others stood a few steps away watching and covering him with their weapons. They were just kids.

"Come on Heinrich," said one of them impatiently, "let's get it over with. Let's get rid of these bandits and be on our way."

Heinrich walked back to his companions.

Thoughts raced through my head, it was war, no court or judges, our chances were slim. We killed them or they killed us. It was their turn. Should I run?

My companions prayed out loud:

"Almighty God, walking through your green pastures, receive our miserable souls, and help our country to be free."

Heinrich lined up with his comrades who had their machine guns pointed towards us. They were so sure. They had us.

"They are sadistic," I thought. Taking their sweet time, I closed my eyes and started to dream.

*

The Polish state came into existence in the 10th century. Wars, fights and disagreements mark the history of Poland, a country located in the most vunerable spot of Europe. Poland was always a pawn between two powers, Russia and Germany, as they are called today. Poland had been divided and absorbed by others countless times. It is incredible that in spite of its internal struggles (i.e. constant oppression of the peasants and the long domination of feudalism), Poland had emerged as a reasonably united country. In the years after World War One, the country was not accustomed to self-rule. Too much division, internal fighting and disagreements created an atmosphere of mistrust where nobody cooperated. It was politically unstable until Marshall Jozef Pilsudski formed a "benevolent" military dictatorship, the year I was born, 1926, between the First and the Second World Wars.

At this time Poland enjoyed twenty years as a free nation after one hundred and twenty three years under foreign rule. Life was beautiful for the privileged. We were a part of that group because my father was attached to the military as an engineer. Writers, musicians and artists also fluorished. The country continued to prosper.

My family consisted of my father Stefan, my mother Anna, an eight-year-older brother Roman and myself, a young school boy.

2

Cherished by family, relatives, friends and the Church, my preschool years were also happy and secure. My earliest memories are of sitting in our apartment window in Warszawa, capital of Poland, from which I could see the "Lotnisko Mokotowskie" [Mokotow Airport], a place where small airplanes usually twin-winged, took off and made intricate aerobatic exercises right over my head. I made childish sketches of the planes which I would proudly display to my parents.

Our next apartment faced a park where the children could play in the small hills and the trees.

An orderly assigned to help "Tatus" [Dad] lived in our tiny kitchen and slept on a folding cot. His main job was polishing my father's boots and keeping his uniform in good shape. "Tatus" had a beautiful full length sabre with a slight bend, while part of the handle was carved in white ivory and encrusted with silver. The blade was inscribed with a motto in a foreign language. Before Christmas the orderly would polish it for long hours shining it to perfection. My father said that it had belonged to his great grandfather who won it during a war with the Turks and the sabre had stayed in the family all these years.

We also had a maid who lived with us. She cleaned the house, cooked and did the laundry. The maid was an illiterate, uneducated country girl who had come to the city to learn a few things and earn a living. The kitchen had a large, coal-burning cooking stove and we often ran down to the basement with a bucket to bring up some coal.

"Alex,"my mother's voice would ring in the air, "please get me a bucket of coal, RIGHT NOW!"

Life was not always rosy. We also had bed bugs, a common pest in those days. They came at night through the ventilation ducts and along the walls. Small, round, brown creatures the size of a small finger nail, promenading on our bodies in the darkness and feasting on our blood. The best way to kill them was to squeeze them between the thumb nails. One had to be careful though not to kill them near the white bed sheets. Filled to the brink with blood they were like small balloons, making an awful mess when they burst. The smell was terrible.

The apartment consisted of a long entrance hallway with doors on both sides. The most interesting room was called "gabinet Tatusia," Dad's little study with a big, dark carved oak desk with lots of papers on it and shelves with many books. Occasionally, we were allowed to play there. I remember one day playing with some friends under the desk in "gabinet Tatusia". We were pretending to be pirates and I put my chewing gum over one of my eyes to look like a vicious pirate. It stuck to my eyelashes and my Mom had a hard time getting it off. My "Tatus" disciplined me by slapping me across my face in front of my friends.

"Tatus" was also a dreamer. In a large windowsill in the dining room my father had a collection of cacti, about twenty species. "Tatus" and I would sit through the night waiting for a specific cactus to bloom.

"This particular one blooms every one hundred years," he said one evening. "If you would like you can sit with me and wait, it looks like it might bloom tonight." So we sat and I fell asleep listening to a distant radio station. In the morning when I got up I ran to the living room. There was the lovely open bloom, yellow with black speckles. I bent to smell it but the scent was unpleasant, something like rotten eggs.

"Every man should have a hobby," said my "Tatus" when he explained to me that the cacti were among the slowest growing plants on earth. People who collected them had to have a great deal of patience.

I cherish the memories of a traditional Polish Christmas dinner which featured pike as the main course. This was the most important among the twelve obligatory dishes. Each Christmas Eve we would go to the market to our own merchant who brought in all kinds of fish. Our chosen pike would weigh at least three pounds and we would take it home wrapped in

4

wet newspapers. We were allowed to keep it for a little while and so we filled the bathtub with cold water and carefully submerged the monster. After a minute or two, the fish would come to life again and vigorously swim back and forth. Quite often it was so large that it had difficulty turning around. We watched it in fascination and its big sharp teeth scared us. Then it disappeared to the kitchen and the next time we saw it it was on the Christmas table submerged in a stiff vegetable jelly. It was served full size on a large oval silver platter.

Polish and International Trade Shows were organized regularly. Once in a while we were allowed to go to such a trade show. My most memorable was the year the new, so-called Superheterodyne, radios were displayed. They could bring in stations from distant places with music, talk-shows and the news. I was most impressed.

* * *

Another great memory from my childhood was a class school trip to the Swietokrzyskie Mountains, 200 kilometres south of Warszawa. We took a train ride and walked upward through a lush, green forest. Higher up, where the trees thinned out, there were a number of smooth, vertical boulders scattered around. According to legend these boulders were the pilgrim-monks who were climbing up to the shrine located at the top of the hill, when by some terrible force, they were turned into stone and were able to move ahead only the length of one tiny grain of sand each year. It is said that when they reach the holy place above, it would be the end of the world and the Judgment Day. Later that day, higher up in the mountain peaks we arrived at a chalet. To this day, I remember the wild strawberries with cream and sugar we had there.

I still have a picture taken on February 8th, 1937 at "Szkola Powszechna na Mokotowie" [Elementary School in Mokotow, Warszawa]. The photographer had a tray extended on a stick high above his head and told us to freeze while he lit the magnesium powder which produced a big flash of light and a puff of smoke. This picture was taken for a New Year, called in Poland "Sylvester," costume party and school play. I liked girls and in the picture I am leaning, in my new sailor' suit, toward a pretty girl standing beside me. On the back of this treasured photo is my father's beautiful handwriting "Carnival in school, 8.II.1937". Every letter was a masterpiece in itself ! Only twice in my life have I seen anyone have such a command of penmanship. One was my "Tatus", the other was a Russian prisoner of war somewhere in northern Finland. When I turn the class picture over and look at the handwriting of my "Tatus", memories from long bygone days fill my head. Such and other memories of my childhood years have remained very precious to me.

Chapter 2

CLOUDS BEFORE THE STORM

I was a member of the Polish Scouting Movement "ZHP"and I chose to be in a section of an Air Troop. It specialized in activities related to flying.

One activity I remember was when for the first time we were marched with the whole group to the black, tall, metal tower. We all climbed up and were strapped to an open parachute. We jumped down as our parents and other people watched. The parachute was attached with a line to the tower so we would not be injured. I enjoyed the jump but got quite dizzy climbing up the open stairs. A thin pipe railing protected me from falling, but nothing could protect me from my view of the ground through the stairs. My heart nearly stopped upon realizing that I was fifty feet above the ground. After our return to the school basement, we formed a "line-up" for debriefing. I fainted and fell down. That is how I knew that the floor was made of stone tiles. What a delayed reaction.

Now we were listening to the radio and to the disturbing reports about Hiltler! There was talk of the armament build-up in Nazi Germany. By

September 1938, Hitler's propaganda campaign of lies and threats was loud and clear. He demanded that the parts of Czechoslovakia that were predominantly German should be incorporated into the Third Reich.

Every Saturday, the whole family sat in front of the radio, listening to entertainment programs from the city of Lwow only to be interrupted by political news. The feeling was that our heroic Polish army was unbeatable. Many of the entertainers made fun of Hitler and Germany. How little we knew what was coming.

In Poland, the anti-Semitic policies existed in the statements of some of the political factions of the government. However, unlike Germany, Poland never had an official government policy against the Jews, however opinions expressed by adults often influenced children. Some of the guys I knew in my school decided to harass the Jews. I went with them to a local synagogue to throw stones and break a large ornate window. Fortunately, the caretakers were alert; as soon as we appeared they came running from behind the stone fence, shouting and waving their arms. We fled as if the devil were on our heels. That was not enough excitment and the hard-heads would not stop. We went to a kiosk and bought a bundle of film strips. They were made of celluloid, leftovers from Hollywood films, a highly inflammable material. A strip, usually about 12 centimeter long was rolled into a tight little tube and wrapped in a small piece of newspaper. When the tube was ignited with a match, it would smoulder not burn, but produce lots of dense smoke. These stink-bombs were thrown into apartments and stores owned by Jews.

After that experience I never travelled with those boys again. I did not see any sense in this type of harassment. Jewish people, with their long hair and curly sideburns, black coats and hats, looked different. Many of them were merchants and they were being accused by the Poles of taking advantage of those less educated. Most Jews, however, were highly learned, knowledgeable and good business people. So, a kind of jealousy must have played a certain role.

My half-brother Roman, at twenty one, was bright and very good looking. His biological father lived in a castle but was killed in a hunting accident. From his father, Roman inherited the title "Hrabia" ("Hr."), meaning "Count." Tall and slim, he walked with the distinction of the nobility. His hands were slim, his bushy dark hair shining almost blue. (People who for generations inherited a certain style, class, courage and other manifestations often thought to belong exclusively to the upper class, and indeed they were different). Roman's widowed mother, evicted from the castle, remarried and became my Mom - thus I have come to this world.

Roman and I did not have much in common as brothers. It was not only the age difference but also the feeling that my father hated Roman. He did not encourage us to be friends. Mother loved us both. Secretly, I was very proud of my older brother. "Tatus" did not like to hear about him. Mom was a wise person, she would make up stories to cover some of our misbehaviour. She had to do this in order to pacify "Tatus", who was very strict. He freely used his belt or a slap across the face. I got spanked many a time and so did Roman; he probably more often than I.

Roman escaped the family pressures by joining the Corps of Cadets as a member of the Military Academy. He dreamed of becoming a career officer. His departure brought a kind of peace to the family.

One day, a heartbreaking news arrived. Something tragic had happened. My parents were summoned to the Academy. Roman's plane had crashed; my mother always suspected sabotage by German agents provocateur. Roman and one of his collegues were dead.

The funeral was conducted with full military honors. The procession to the cemetery was led by the Air Force Band, followed by a priest dressed in white, then the relatives and Air Force officers. The grave site was beautiful. Each of the two graves had a big cross with a wooden aeroplane propeller attached to them. I loved looking at them and the shape of the propellers fascinated me. Mass was celebrated in a grand, old stone church adjacent to the cementary. I do not remember the church mass, but I remember a woman screaming at the grave site. I vividly recall the other fellow's mother jumping up from her chair and throwing herself across the casket of her son. She cried out loudly and horribly: "My son, my poor son, why were you taken from us?"

My mother explained to me later that we should not manifest such gestures publicly. I learned the lesson that grief should be expressed privately. I missed my brother terribly. Only after his death did I discover that we had lots in common. Somehow we had not developed a brotherly relationship. In 1993 in Warszawa, I visited the cemetery. The propeller was gone but the marble stone still reads:

Hr. ROMAN BROCHWICZ, Polish pilot
died in 1939

I still honour my brother, my hero.

Chapter 3

SEPTEMBER 1st, 1939

We had been listening to the radio and knew that there was a possibility of a war with Germany. I was 100% sure, together with millions of others, that the Germans would not invade Poland. If they dared, our great Polish Air Force and Army with its numerous famous cavalry divisions would easily defeat those aggressive Germans. We were ready to show them off.

One night we heard some unusual noise, shooting and explosions. Being young, and excited about going to my new high school, I did not pay much attention.

Friday morning, after the church service mother went home to prepare dinner, "Tatus" asked me to walk with him to Lotnisko Mokotowskie, the nearby civil airport. We strolled along the Aleja Niepodleglosci [Independence Boulevard] one of the most modern streets in the area. The boulevard was divided in the middle with a grassed median and finished with expertly laid

square granite stones. It was often used for parades because of its double lanes and the wide pavement. We passed the last buildings and found ourselves in the open space of the airport. A little distance ahead, on the median, an old, rusty iron tower stood about twenty feet tall. In earlier years it had a wind-sleeve and other navigational gadgets. When the modern boulevard was built, the hangars and the equipment were relocated further to the west, but somehow the tower remained. As we approached the iron structure we saw some large holes in the median beside the tower. They were four or five feet deep and freshly "dug", or so I thought. We crossed to the center to look at them more closely. My father ran his fingers over the rusty iron structure of the tower and pointed out some of the holes in the heavy iron. The holes were bent out and had shiny sharp edges, newly made and not rusted like the rest of the structure.

"The war has started," said my "Tatus". "We must go home right away and cover all our windows. I've got some glue and tape and you will have to help me." He briskly turned around and quickly started for home. I had a hard time keeping up with him. Thousands of questions ran through my head. Breathlessly running beside him I asked: "Tatus, those holes in the ground, they weren't from bombs or something like that, were they?" "Tatus" did not know what to say, he did not want to terrify me but he had to be honest. "Yes," he said, "I think the Germans have started to invade Poland."

As soon as we got home "Tatus" took my mother into the next room and sent me to get something from the store. On the way I wondered if the air attack alarm that sounded last night was real or practise? Needing a second opinion, I quickly ran to my friend's apartment. Adam's mother opened the door and I saw her packing big suitcases. "Where is Adam?" I asked. Standing in the doorway and politely taking off my new possession - my high school cap - I waited for her answer. "I have sent him to get my husband. It would be ridiculous to stay in the city when the Germans are about to attack! We will be much better off in the country," she said in a high pitched voice.

"So, you mean the Germans are attacking?" I asked with some excitment. I had just turned 13 and did not yet understand the seriousness of the situation.

"Yes, did you not listen to the radio? Two nights ago they crossed the Polish border and are moving quickly toward Warszawa. We will not stay here and get slaughtered like pigs. We would be much safer in our country cottage on the other side of the Wisla River." I heard what she said but I found it odd that people I had known all my life would just pack up and go.

My parents were preparing to stay. When I arrived home, they were moistening and gluing paper strips on all of our windows. Even the kitchen window was not spared.

Preparation for war started at once. We were called out to the park square in front of our apartment. All the people, young and old, were asked to bring a shovel and to start digging trenches. These were dug in a zig-zag pattern and were about seven feet deep. The trenches were to be used by everybody, in case of heavy bombardment. If you were in the trenches, even close explosions would not harm you. Within hours the trenches had been dug.

That afternoon there were a couple air attack alarms and some explosions were heard. At first people ran to the ditches for protection, Since it was rather difficult to climb in and out of the trenches, people quickly stopped using them.

The following afternoon "Tatus" came home in a "company car," a military vehicle driven by a chauffeur. They unloaded gas-masks, several blankets and a whole pile of jute bags. Shortly afterwards we started to fill them up with sand and earth. These sandbags were to be used on the roof and in the stairwells of the building in case a bomb started a fire. We also received a couple of cases of "iron rations," a form of a pea soup with meat in green painted cans. These Polish "iron rations" did not taste too bad and during the siege of Warszawa, when food was scarce, they were a treasure to have. I did not know the name of this food in Poland but a few years later I heard similar rations being described in Norway, where it was was called the "Dead Man."

The air attacks of Warszawa intensified. One day we went downtown to visit some friends. While the grown-ups were talking, I went down to the street to a "piekarnia" [bakery] to buy some cakes. Fortunately at that time they were still available. When standing in line in the crowded bakery, a nice looking, blond, young man ahead of me, said, "I would like some of these CIASTKI." Suddenly, the crowd became totally quiet. There was a tense silence. Only a small boy somewhere nervously shuffled his feet on the marble floor. You could hear a pin drop.

Immediately, a man in plain clothes moved quickly toward the fellow, pulled a gun and shouted "Hands up, this is the police." The blond man reluctantly raised his hands and was searched by the "tajniak" [undercover

agent]. A Luger, a big German 9 MM pistol was found on the young man, stuck through his belt. The agent handcuffed him immediately. The policeman excused himself to the customers explaining that he had captured one of the German spies who had been sent ahead of the invading armies to sabotage our defences. What the fellow had done was mispronounce the plural for cookies saying CIASTKI instead of CIASTKA. After all this excitement I got my box of delicious cream cakes. (Of all the places in the world, they are still the best in Warszawa.) I ran as fast as I could, taking three or four steps at a time to tell everybody what I had just witnessed.

While we were visiting, the air alarm sounded and we all hurried to the basement. I hid in the stairway until the booming voice of my mother summoned me down on the double. I got a glimpse of a Junkers 87 (Stuka) dive-bomber attacking something a few blocks away. A long, wailing siren announced the air-raid was over. Daily life returned to normal. We could through from the windows that the chaos caused by the recent bombing did not affect the pulse of the city The streets were crowded again. We took the tram home to the Mokotow quarter of Warszawa.

On a sunny afternoon as the bombardment of Warszawa by the advancing German troops continued, the radio broadcast a speech by

14

"burmistrz" [The Mayor], Stefan Starzynski. He proudly announced the names of a heroic crew of a heavy machine gun who had shot down an enemy plane. The announcement came just minutes after the incident.

Since the location was close by, we all ran down to the open field where dozens of people of all sizes and ages who together lifted up the broken wing. I will never forget the beautiful light blue color on the underside of the wings, a camouflage technique the Germans were trying. The aeroplane, a fighter, hit the ground with enormous force, ripping off the wings which were made of light aluminum. The pilot must have been killed in the air. He had somehow managed to switch off the engine, since there had been no explosion or fire. People were all over the aircraft wreck, climbing, tearing, unscrewing pieces, chopping pieces with pocket knifes and even bare hands. They were tearing at it in a frenzy. Some of the more eager souvenir hunters were bleeding from cuts but still laughing and shouting. Everybody wanted a souvenir. It was an unbelieveable sight. I was curious, and since I had not yet learned to enjoy the death of an enemy, my imagination took over, giving life to the dead pilot.

Karl was young and eager. Approaching the capital of Poland with his squadron of eight speedy fighters he was thinking of his home in the little village of Malderburg, not far from Hamburg, where his mother and his fiance were waiting for his return. He had been on steady attack for the last three weeks and it was his turn tomorrow to go back home for a brief ten days visit to see family and to get married to his lovely Gertruda.

So far, there had been little resistance from the Polish army as the German Blitzkrieg progressed with enormous speed. It was almost like war exercises, with simulated mass killing of troops and civilians. He was glad that the siege would be over as his great German army continued the victories of the first days.

"Fan out and start straffing larger buildings," came the rapid command on his radio. "Red three [that was him], turn 30° left and aim toward that church tower ahead of you."

"Jawohl," answered Karl dutifully and immediately started to turn his machine in the direction pointed out. It was then that he felt an enormous pain in his stomach and blacked out thinking "What is happening to me?" In a few brief seconds his aflame fighter started to spiral down toward the earth.

Suddenly my eyes focused on the body of the pilot, still strapped into his seat. I watched it being dragged to the ground. He was a nice looking young man not much older than I. Blood drenched his stomach through his pilot's overalls. My eyes got blurry and again I started to visualize the pilot's life, his childhood and....

"Karl, how was school today?" It was a sunny afternoon in the village of Malderburg. Karl came home from school, a little late, because of the obligatory meeting of the Hitler Jugend group where they practised shooting with real guns, and memorized the doctrines of the new, wonderful Fuehrer, Adolf Hitler.

"OK, Mum. Sorry I am late but you know the Hitler Jugend, we have to practise and practise.

"What did you do today?" asked his mother.

"Oh the usual, we competed in sharp shooting and Herr Jodler told us about the horrible Polacks who do not allow German citizens in Poland to buy property or travel freely where they want. Herman told me that this is not exactly true, because he just came back from visiting his uncle in Radom. His uncle has started a small business producing cigarette boxes and is doing quite well".

"Yes, to be honest with you, I do not always agree with all the stories we are told."

"Mom, be careful. Somebody might report you and you will be in big trouble."

"Wanna a piece of that cursed plane, kid?" said a voice beside me. An outstretched hand held a small piece of thin aluminum painted bright blue on one side.

"Thanks, that is very nice of you," I replied staring at the piece of cold metal in my hand.

From the left: the author, pseudonym "Olek", Jurek Horczak "Wrobel" and Andrzej Bledowski "Bury".

Chapter 4

FOOD AND FIRE

By September 8th, the German ground forces surrounded Warszawa. Their big cannons bombarded the city. Air attacks by the dive-bombers, most often Stukas 87, the planes with the comical bent-up wings, were endless. The assaults caused a 24 hour non-stop destruction. The alarm sirens signaled new attacks even before the long signal for OVER sounded. The Germans were in a tight circle all around the city waiting for orders to take Warszawa. The brave Polish cavalry was no match for a modern, mechanized army. We had a number of planes but they were outdated and the Germans made sure that most of them were destroyed immediately either by sabotage or by bombing the airports. The defense, consisting mostly of troops who had withdrawn to the city from other fronts were continuing to hold out in the hope of support from Western allies.

By the second week of the invasion we were getting starving. No stores were open, very few people wandered the streets. Much of time we

spent in the safety of the basement. Not that the stinky old hole, built like a brick catacomb with an earthen floor, provided any security. I saw many people buried in their basement when a direct hit collapsed the entire building. Between the alarms we would run upstairs to our once warm and cozy apartment, the wooden parquet floors were now rough and scratched from all the shattered glass and debris. It was September and the weather became chilly. Blankets and cardboard replaced the window panes. As my father looked outside between the torn blankets in the window, he saw a freshly killed horse just outside our building. "Tatus", with the courage borne of hunger, ran out with a big butcher knife. Mom pulled me away from the window and spared me the view of what was happening.

The supper, although interrupted by another air attack alarm, was very tasty. The horse meat was tough, but it had the flavour of fried meat and its rather sweetish taste did not stop our hungry stomachs from wanting more.

The evening was unusually quiet so we went outside to look around. The horse's cadaver was still there. People were lined up haggling and swearing at each other while trying to get a piece of the meat. As a result of "Tatus" quick reaction, we were not as hungry as we otherwise would have been.

The German attacks intensified by day and night but the defenders of our capital were extremely brave and held the invaders at bay. Although our Polish held territory was shrinking by the hour there was no sign of giving up. Not yet.

One reasonably quiet morning, Mother and I walked to my elementary school further up at Narbutta Street. We had not been out for several days. What met our eyes was horrifying; buildings destroyed, fires smoldering, and people digging through the ruins. We didn't know whether they were looking for family and friends or for possessions in the bombed buildings. As we neared the school - a cannon barrel was suddenly pointing straight at us. It was green and the hole was black and ominous, full of death! I couldn't believe my eyes. This big, green, frightening machine on two rubber tires was being readied to fire. A couple of Polish soldiers yelled and warned us: "Get off the street immediately!"

In the panic we ran into the school building. The school seemed empty. Down in the big basement, where we normally used to have our Scout meetings, something strange was going on. We saw some extra tables, a group of nurses and white clad doctors. Our school was now a field hospital. People were running in and out. In the yard we could see that a field kitchen had been erected. A bunch of fatigue clad soldiers were cooking meals. It seemed like I was caught in the middle of some bizarre play watching people change the props.

While we were standing in the basement talking to some people, a teacher joined in our conversation. Suddenly there was a tremendous explosion right outside the windows, another and another. Curiosity made me run up the main stairway towards the central entrance doors. The heavy oak, stained glass doors had exquisite stained-glass that had been covered with some old plywood. Through the holes in the plywood I saw the cannon. Right in front of the entrance it was firing down the street in the direction from which we had just come. The noise was overwhelming. The soldiers were rhythmically loading new shells and after the command "Ognia!" [Fire!], the whole cannon would spit flames and jump a little off the ground. After a few rounds they stopped shooting. Fortunately, the shelling was not returned by the invaders. Through the peep-hole I saw the soldiers bring a horse from a side street and hitch it to the cannon to pull it away. I ran downstairs to report all the news.

We headed home. The cannon shells must have gone much further than the few blocks we had to walk home. We could not see any marks. The street trees were still intact and there were no holes in the pavement. They must have been shooting at some distant German positions.

The air alarm sirens started to wail again as we walked along.

"Hurry up," said mom, "we had better run a little." So we did. We just made it home when we could hear the first wave of Stukas approaching. They dive bombed here and there. The Germans were mad. It took them longer than they thought. They were no more selecting just military targets. I sneaked up to the roof of our three store building to get a better view. When the bombing and shooting seemed to have moved away from us, others came to join me on the roof. Many of the sandbags "Tatus" had supplied at the beginning of the war were now fully utilized. They were laid on the roof in rows, both along the entrance and at the edges, ready to be used in case of fire.

The Germans, in addition to their regular exploding bombs, were using small, incendiary bombs. These were little tubes about half a meter long, with fins at one end. The bombs did not explode, but upon impact burst into intense hot flames. Hundreds of these were dropped every day and if people did not spot them and neutralize them with shovels full of sand, they would start roof or shed fires. Once ignited, they were almost impossible to extinguish. Some of them did not ignite, just like the ones that fell in our backyard. I lifted one up one day and wanted to keep it as a souvenir. "Tatus" said that it was too risky, so we buried the bomb in the backyard.

Half the city was burning. Everywhere we looked there were fires. Viewing all that destruction,

I recalled long, long time ago a vacation in the village of Jezioro. One day, the big clouds had gathered on the horizon and a powerful thunder storm swept over the area. We, children, were sitting in the deep windows of the farmhouse, admiring the spectacle and watching cascades of water form a river going down the sandy road in front of the house, when somebody shouted "Fire!" By that time the rain was almost over and we all ran barefoot to the street wading in the warm streams of water running down the road. At the end of the street a barn was on fire. Thick billows of smoke were coming from the straw roof and the farmer, whose cow barn was attached to the same building, was leading two cows out. Many neighbors came running with buckets and formed a line to the water well. The young fellows hauling water up from the well worked as fast as they could but the barn burned down. Fortunately, the fire did not spread. Early next morning the neighbors began to arrive with donations for the unfortunate family. Within a few days, after removing the ashes and twisted iron fittings, a group of people started to build a new barn.

But now, I was back in the middle of the burning Warszawa. Some fires looked smaller than others but there were too many of them. The air was saturated with a horrible stench of burning rags, garbage and decomposing bodies.

The end of an air alarm sounded, an even tone lasting three minutes. As we returned to the apartment to make tea, another air alarm started. It's undulating tone announced the attacking planes. So we ran to the basement to try and seek some safety. We had no rest from this ordeal . For four weeks, this went on and on for four weeks until the fierce Polish resistance was crushed.

FAMILY PHOTO
First from left (standing) Roman, mother (in white) holding the author, dad in uniform.

23

Chapter 5

THE IRON FIST

On September 28, 1939 the siege of Warszawa ended, the city capitulated. Much of the city was in ruins, people and animals buried under the destroyed buildings. Smoke as well as the stench of decomposing bodies permeated the air.

The Germans staged a victory parade on Aleja Niepodleglosci [Independence Boulevard]. It was a sunny day in Mokotow, a southwestern district of Warszawa where we lived. Our neighbourhood was not damaged as much as many other districts. People came from everywhere. Most of them, for the past weeks, had been hiding in basements or bomb shelters. People reacted in different ways. Some were grateful for the fresh air and the sound of silence, others were bandaged, many were crying. They had already been through hell and had no concept of their future. Young mothers with strollers presented a contrasting picture to the scene of gloom and despair.

The "Uber Rasse" (master race, as the Germans thought of themselves) was arrogant. The banner, a big flat flag with an embroidered eagle holding a swastika, led the parade. A marching band played "Heil - li... Heil-lu" ["Valleri ...Vallera"] and the marching soldiers sang the "Ha - ha - ha - ha" with gusto! A big, white, strong horse, carried a high ranking officer wearing a helmet. He was followed by marching columns of soldiers, tanks and artillery. Adolf Hitler, himself, was inspecting the same parade just a few blocks from us but we did not know it at that time.

There were a few people among the spectators waving small swastika flags. They must have been early civilian arrivals or people of German origin living in Poland. The "Volksdeutsche" were ready to receive their comrades.

I noticed some people had turned their backs on the parade and pretended to be talking to somebody behind them. In the early days of occupation the Germans did not respond to that type of silent disdain. To my horror, I saw a man lower his pants and underwear and expose his bare ass to the marching troops. Fortunately he was not in the front row and none of the enemy saw him. I imagined what would have happened, if they had.

We went home with mixed feelings. It was a relief that the fighting was over and the shelling had stopped. As we were never exposed to the front line of combat, my family had not suffered as much as others and we did not die of starvation. What the future was going to bring us about we did not know. How long would this war last? Would the Allies, come to Poland's aid and defeat the German occupiers? Warszawa had fought heroically for 28 days, but was rendered helpless against the superior technology of the German army.

I wondered why German troops were here in the first place? Where were the British, the French who declared war on Germany already on September 3rd, and all the other allies who had been criticizing Germany? America was not at war at that time so there was no hope of help from them. I was sure that any day now the British would start real war on Germany. What were they waiting for?

Immediately after the invasion, Germany annexed Poland's Western Provinces, about one quarter of the entire country with the intent that these territories would be completely Germanized. Occupied Central Poland was put under rule of a German Governor General. Poles in the area were to be allowed to follow their own customs under the direction of the German Reich. This intent lasted less than a month before the Governor General began closing universities, newspaper offices and cultural institutions in an effort to wipe out Polish society. Poland's eastern territory, taken by the Soviets, was under the rule of the Soviet Russia (USSR).

* * *

Shortly after, in 1940, the word QUISLING became known all over the world as a replacement of the word

TRAITOR...

To make a long story short, Norway, like many other Europoean countries, was captured by surprise by the Germans. The Norwegian King and government escaped safely to England, but a Norwegian man, named Quisling, formed a new government under the German rule. Desperately, during the five years of war, he tried to induce the population of his country to follow him, but with no success. Norway became the country most opposed to the German occupation. The Norwegians had their own, strong Underground Movement which sabotaged the enemy at every opportunity. Immediately after the war, Quisling was arrested and sentenced to death.

During the German occupation of Poland, Poles formed no government under the German rule; only the Underground Delegature of the Polish Government-in-Exile in London was recognized and obeyed by the Polish people. We had never produced a Quisling.

This notwithstanding, at the end of the war which was unconditionally won by the Allies, Poland was not actually liberated. After the war victorious to others, for forty-five yeas, Poland stayed under the communist domination. As the rest of the world enjoyed peace and freedom, Poland was pushed around by the gruesome NKVD [Soviet Secret Police]. Soviet Russia had total control over my country. My dream of a free Poland was not realized until the 1989 break-up of this totalitarian system and of the Soviet Union itself.

* * *

After the capitulation of Warszawa on September 28th, 1939, life in Poland would never be the same. The active aggression had stopped, but German imposed terror was instituted. Nevertheless, life, in a way, started to return to normal.

My new high school, however, was different. A school yard full of new faces, everybody wearing the new high school cap. I was so proud of mine. The next day we finally began high school. My friends and I were excited about going to school and learning again. A Polish teacher spoke to us first in a way which was totally different from that we had been spoken to in elementary school.

"Ladies and Gentlemen, you are no longer small children in a primary school. You are young and vibrant men and women, almost adults now, and I command you to act accordingly. Your future rests in your own hands. Nobody can promise you higher education, health and riches. Only you can decide what you want to be on this earth and only you can achieve the goals you set for yourself." We sat spellbound.

In those days students respected the law, teachers and older people. We respected our elders for the wisdom which we assumed they all had. We also believed in great opportunities in life. We believed the future would bring us things beyond our dreams. We hoped we would live in a better world lead by wise and kindly people. Stealing and cheating were acts committed by the uneducated, those who lived in poverty and who grew up in an environment of basic survival. Little did we know that soon we would become accomplished liars, thieves and killers.

The Principal called a general meeting. All the classes assembled in the gymnasium, the doors flew open with a bang and two uniformed German guards marched in. They were not alone. They were body guards for a big fellow, a typical Gestapo agent, who wore the obligatory hat, and epaulets on his coat and had his hands stuffed in his pockets.

"Ladies and Gentlemen," said the Principal "I have been asked to introduce this gentleman, Sigmund Koch. Herr Koch has a few little things to announce." Sigmund Koch clearly enjoyed his prominence. He took his time and after careful clearing his throat, he spoke in a broken Polish:

"Young people of Poland, you are now living in a country that under the wise guidance of the Third Reich will become a great country."

To accomplish this fabulous greatness, the Germans (who wanted more workers than academics from Poland) allowed us to get a limited education under certain conditions.

"Every youth, in addition to his academic training, must also learn a trade," continued Herr Koch. "Therefore, I hereby declare, that you will be allowed to continue your education in this school under one condition. You must chose a manual profession, and alternate, one week in a workshop, one week in the school." He made it clear that if anyone objected, he would be expelled from school and sent to a labour camp.

With his message delivered the fellow clicked his heels and shouted:

"Heil Hitler," jerking his arm in a funny way forward. With his two companions, he stiftly marched out.

The students reacted with tremendous noise which lasted for a few minutes. Everyone was shouting and arguing. Our Principal stepped forward and silenced the crowd.

"Listen, this is not a joke. They are very serious. We have no choice, do we? Look at this positively. It is quite often very handy to know something about a trade."

I chose auto repair. I was sent down town to a busy auto repair shop. The work stalls were in a row along one wall, some had dugouts, some did not. I do not recall if they had lifts at that time. We had German bosses and the shop mostly serviced the vehicles of the German administration in Warszawa. I was assigned to a mechanic and became his handy man and helper. We all got coveralls supplied by the company, and ten small brass disks with numbers on them. These had a hole and were threaded on a safety pin which we attached to our coverall.These were "proofs of identity," required when we borrowed tools from the tool wicket in the shop.

One day, the mechanic, Herr Rafter, to whom I was assigned, was repairing a carburetor which had small parts, and relatively small screws. "Alex," he shouted, "I need a wrench to finish fixing this carburetor. Go to the tool wicket and get me one." I did not realize that all the others were aware of what was going to happen, they were standing along the repair stalls, pretending to work but looking at me to see what would come next. I went to the tool wicket.

"Please give me the 'Schlussel' [a wrench], because Herr Rafter is repairing a carburetor," I said as I exchanged one of my disks to get the tool. I was given the biggest wrench key I had ever seen. Being inexperienced, I did not know what wrench I should have been given. What the two men brought out I could not carry. It was too big. I had to drag it past all the stalls while people laughed.

Herr Rafter laughed the most.

"What have you brought me?" he taunted.

"This is the key to repair axles not carburetors, ha...ha...ha...ha...who the hell gave you that one.... ha.... ha?"

I was not content in the auto shop, not because of their sense of humor but because I did not find auto repair very interesting. For example, we, the beginners, had to attach a small piece of metal in a vise and file it with a big, flat file to try to make a perfect cube. This seemed to me to be a useless task. There was not enough challenge in auto repairs to keep me interested. I became an electrician apprentice. I was assigned to a master electrician who had a job in a steam locomotive workshop. It was an enormous hall with a very high ceiling. Every morning the apprentices had to climb several high ladders to the top. In a thick layer of dust and dirt, on narrow gangways, we had to replace old, half rotten wires with new 500 Volt ones. This was a slow and dangerous job. We worked with fairly high voltage and I often had to balance on narrow planks, high above the locomotives and work with different tools and wires.

"Hand me that roll of wire, Alex, and be careful," said my foreman one day. The gangways were a tricky place, you did not know if you were stepping on a solid plank or on a piece of cardboard. The years of accumulated dust covered everything evenly, and I was not careful enough... I slipped on some grease on the dust covered gangway and fell, but got caught around my waist by a steel line supporting a fuse box. So, I hung forty feet above the floor, my arms and legs dangling. I looked down and was staring right into a locomotive's funnel ten feet below me. The smoke was puffing right at me. I could have sworn that I saw the fire in the belly of that big, black monster.

An alarm sounded, something like "man overboard."

"Hang in there, Alex, don't move too much so that the line does not give up. Hold tight!," yelled my boss. It was easier said than done. My legs were getting hot from the billowing smoke under me.

It took three men half an hour to lower a line and pull me up. It was scary, my heart pounded, but it was not my time yet. I did not know then that this training would save my life later. I received an Ausweis [ID card] which stated that I was an electrician.

Chapter 6

THE UNDERGROUND

A secret meeting in our apartment had been called by the scout leaders. My parents were not aware of what was happening. We were trying to form a small resistance group. We gathered in the dining room and one of the leaders opened a large parcel. He pulled out a giant, German flag. It was red with a white circle and a black swastika in the center. We all spread the enormous piece of heavy linen on the floor, like a carpet. Then we walked on it, first gingerly and then with heavy, trampling steps, our feet burned with justice. This symbolized that the Germans, despite occupying our country, had not taken control of our spirits and hearts. We listened to a short history of Poland and its Constitution. We were made to swear that we would fight for our country until death. At that moment, I became an underground soldier and joined the Allied war effort, facing the reality of death.

One of the leaders produced a REAL pistol, loaded with LIVE ammunition. I could not believe my eyes; it seemed exciting to a 14-year old. For the next couple of hours we received our first lesson on small weapons. We all had to hold the gun, take it apart and put it together again. We learned that we should never, ever point a weapon at anyone, even if unloaded, unless we did intend to kill. They demonstrated to us how to draw it quickly from under our belts. All the time, I was wondering what would happen should the gun went off. My hands were sweating.

As the weeks passed our lessons continued and we were taught the use of all kinds of weapons, including hand grenades. I was excited about being a member of the Underground Army, but I was also very, very scared. I was given the code name "Olek."

By spring 1940 we were fully engaged in anti-German activities. Most were non violent acts like painting large slogans against the Germans on walls. We painted swastikas on the windows and entrances to the homes of suspected German collaborators and informers. We constructed small hangman gallows to put on the doors of "German Only" restaurants. We scrawled "Deutschland Kaput" on cinemas' walls.

A few times we jumped on our bicycles and rode to a busy downtown street in broad daylight. We pedaled like crazy and because we despised the photos of the smiling German soldiers on display, we threw stones at a Polish photographer's window. We distributed illegally printed news bulletins. We had become aware of the seriousness of the German occupation, the arrests, the executions, the stealing of property and of national treasures. Pre-war Boy-Scouts became perpetrators of minor sabotage, and finally graduated to soldiers performing attacks on the occupying forces.

Once, we received orders to report to a greenhouse. Jurek Horczak, code name "Wrobel" [Sparrow], and I showed up early the next morning. After exchanging the password greetings, we were ushered into a warehouse where we saw several young trees a couple of metres tall. Their trunks and roots were wrapped with rugs and string. We were informed that a Mauser rifle was camouflaged in the wrappings on each sapling. Jurek and I were to deliver two of these to an address across town. We were each given a loaded pistol with an extra clip of ammunition, which were hidden in our belts.

On the street we decided to ride on the front platform of the street car which read "Nur fur Deutsche" [Only for the Germans]. We felt it might be safer in case of a street control and we were confident that we knew enough German to get by.

Carrying our cumbersome loads, we boarded the tram. The Polish section was overcrowded as usual. The front platform had only a couple of uniformed soldiers. With a polite smile they made room for us and our trees. Everything went smoothly until we jumped off the tram while it was still in motion. Horror of horrors, Jurek's pistol fell to the pavement with a bang. No one paid attention to this mishap. People went about their usual business. We were probably mistaken for Germans. Nonchalantly, Jurek replaced his pistol, and we carried on with our trees. The mission was accomplished.

One day it was suggested that we make an explosive device. The telephone company in Warszawa used a hanging conduit which was imbedded in a lead tube. When the thin inner wires were removed, a narrow, very flexible lead tube which was a little thinner than a pencil remained. There were tons of that tubing material available. A five centimeter long piece of the lead tubing was made into an exploding device. One of the famous Polish wooden matches was placed in one end and the tube was crimped around the match stick. That was the tail, the lighter end. The open front end was filled with lots of sulphur scraped from match heads and then the hole was plugged with a small nail. Because the tube was pretty full the nail stuck out a little. This device, thrown or shot with a slingshot, would, upon impact, explode with a loud bang. These miniature bombs did not cause damage or injuries, just a loud explosion.

We produced these bombs for our members whose apartments were close or above a cinema-theatre. It was our wish to scare the movie-goers away. The Germans ran inexpensive shows in order to attract people, who would then be subjected to propaganda newsreels which always preceded the main feature. The underground Home Army did not want people to be brainwashed by this propaganda. A busy campaign of posters and graffiti calling the cinema goers pigs was also mounted. The rhyming slogan read

"Tylko swinie
siedza w kinie"

which meant only pigs go to the movies. We tried to help this campaign by exploding our devices in front of the theatres. Our purpose was to prevent people from going to watch the Third Reich army constantly winning and gloryfying themselves. The small bomb campaign was quite successful and fewer and fewer people went to see the movies. I once heard about a small boy who upon entering the cinema theatre asked loudly his mother, "Mom, where are the pigs?".

We also became quite expert in sling shooting but were maybe a bit cavalier. One day, I was standing in my bedroom in front of a big mirror mixing white nitro and yellow sulphur, two powders cheaper than match heads and available in greater quantities. Holding a lab glass tube in my left hand I was carefully adding a little bit of one powder and a little bit of the other. I was trying to avoid banging the container on the edge of the test tube but somehow failed with loud results.

I did not hear the actual explosion, the sound in my ears changed slowly from a low to a very high pitch. I saw a fireball in front of me. The large mirror shattered and suddenly my face and hands were bleeding profusely. I couldn't hear a thing, only that bloody high pitch. It was a disaster.

My problem was to find a hospital or a doctor who would not inform the Germans. Some friends were called and I was rushed to a "safe" doctor. She was also involved in the underground movement and accepted me without question. A small operation was performed to remove as much glass as possible. It was difficult because the lab tube I was using was made of clear glass and it is not easy to spot pieces of clear glass inside bleeding wounds. Fortunately, all the pieces went into my hand sparing my eyes. I was deaf for three months before my hearing started gradually to return. I learned a most important lesson: "Be extremely careful with all explosives."

Fifteen years later another operation had to be performed at the University Hospital in Oslo, Norway, before I immigrated to Canada. My left hand is full of scars and I cannot press or squeeze it too much. Some glass bits still remain and they sometimes hurt

Orders often came from the Underground for our cell to acquire weapons. Once, we planned to disarm a blue uniformed Polish policeman taking away his VIS, the standard pistol used in the Polish Army and Police Forces. Two of us, shaking in our pants, went downtown. We saw an older policeman enter an apartment building and followed him to a dark staircase. We thought we could just give him a push and grab his gun. We carried no weapons of any kind.

For some reason I've never understood why he reacted to our quiet shadowing. We were unnaturally quiet and this probably made the policeman suspicious. He drew his gun, and marched us to the nearest police station where we were put in a jail cell. The heavy grate sliding doors rolled slowly closed and locked with a loud clang. The sound echoed and echoed in the almost empty cement room.

While the officer was calling our parents, we invented a story to explain our presence in that building. We said that we went to the staircase to get some of the nice sand kept on every floor in big containers, in case of fire. I had a little cage at home in which I was keeping some white mice as a class project, I said, so I decided to get some sand for my mice from the staircase in that building. Our faces looked innocent. Everybody believed our lie and we were freed. It had been a horrifying day. Had we been taken to a German detention centre, the consequences might have been more severe. We realized that if we did not want to sacrifice our lives through stupidity, we would have to plan our underground activities very carefully.

But our next request to acquire weapons had more dramatic consequences. We had targeted a uniformed German whom we had seen returning alone at the same hour each evening to a small house on a darkened street. Equipped with pistols, four of us were to walk at night, shortly before the curfew hour, and force his Luger from him. About 9 o'clock that evening, when it was dark, we started on our mission.

Zbyszek and I were a back-up team walking across the street on the edge of the sidewalk. The German walked towards Jurek and Jacek. We lowered our heads in subservience. Jurek faced him.

"Hande hoch...geben Sie mir Ihre Luger," he said as firmly as his nerves would allow. The soldier, wearing a red armband with swastika on his arm stood very still. The armband looked especially menacing in the dim light as he stared cooly at the two boys facing him.

Nobody moved.

A tense second passed and I was getting my weapon ready. Suddenly, the German jumped to the side and clawed at his holster. We gave a hoarse cry.

I pulled at my pistol but Jurek, facing him on the other side of the street, reacted immediately. He shot the German three times and calmly bent down to remove the Luger pistol from the twitching soldier. He stuck it in his belt and we bolted, running like demons from hell!

The next day, we heard that the Germans had dragged 150 people out of surrounding houses and executed them at the same spot their soldier had fallen.

The thought of so many countrymen and neighbours dying for one soldier and one Luger made our coup seem hollow. Our Scout leader saw our flagging spirits and explained the hard realities.

"If the Underground were to be successful, weapons were necessary. They are obtained at a horrendous price. Every time we take weapons from the Germans, we risk our lives, those of our families and those of innocent civilians. This is war."

Chapter 7

SURVIVAL

The Third Reich continued its European aggression, relying on the resources of their occupied territories. Most of what was produced in Poland was being shipped west to feed the hungry German armies. Their propaganda claimed that they were fighting on all the fronts "to free the world from tyranny." Poland was no longer known as the land of milk and honey. There was very little food available to us Poles and we had to supplement our supplies.

A community garden was established at part of the old Warszawa airport, Lotnisko Mokotowskie. We did not have a parcel of land, but we had some friends who did. From salvaged materials, they built a small hut and furnished it with benches, table and a stove. Their plot of land was divided into small sections. Potatoes were the primary crop, cabbages, carrots and red beets were grown because they could be stored through the winter. My family used to work there for hours and were rewarded with some of the produce. Work helped make people forget the misery of the war. It was a pleasure to be doing something that resulted in an achievement. Gardening was not violent and the effort helped one sleep peacefully at night. Aching muscles somehow give a feeling of accomplishment.

As another method of making money, friends grew small mulberry bushes and fed their leaves to silkworms. The garden had some apple and peach trees. The fruit was a treat each fall as fresh fruit was a luxury. It was divided evenly among all and was used for many, special meals. We did not have refrigerators, only ice boxes, so every thing was checked daily to make sure that nothing edible was spoiled.

Mother used to send me to the store to buy a jar full of sauerkraut in its juice. The food store had little to sell but sauerkraut was usually available. I loved the garlic juice in which it was preserved. We had coupons that had to be used carefully if they were to last the whole month. Our margarine and bread was purchased with these coupons. It was rumored that, under German orders, the bakers added sawdust to the ingredients. This trick allowed for larger quantities of bread dough to be made but the bread tasted very bitter. There was no choice but this heavy, dark bread, no buns and no white bread.

Our kitchen stove was on constantly to prepare tea, coffee or hot milk. Coffee was made from roasted oak tree acorns and it tasted dreadful. We did not have pasteurized milk so it had to be boiled. Often our meals were soups and grain dishes. Once in a long while a piece of fat sausage was available. This was divided into many small portions and used sparingly so it would last for some time.

Our friend's garden during the occupation years saved us not only from starvation but from a poorly balanced diet. Sitting among trees and bushes in the day time, or in the little hut with a kerosene lamp in the evening, one could forget for a few hours the agony of war.

Many stories were told on such evenings, stories about a free Poland. We dreamed about what we would be be doing when the hated Germans were defeated. We played games, talked and listened; the "institution" of "Homegardens" helped keep us sane.

I remember my Mother sending me with some of the garden produce she had carefully hidden in my school book bag, to see an old uncle. He lived in "Stare Miasto," the oldest square in the city. The houses were connected and built like an impressive fortress. The square was laid with cube stone pavement. He lived on the top floor in an attic flat with slanted ceilings. It was a very beautiful, antique building. Inside it smelled of old wood and tar. Because of the tiny windows it was very dark.

I spent the night there. In the morning I said good-bye and thanked my uncle. All the old buildings especially the antique ones, had massive street gates which were always locked at night. I ran down the stairs and stopped in my tracks. I saw a Gestapo patrol next to the building entrance rounding up people. I ran back as fast as I could. I asked my uncle to let me out on the roof through one of the tiny windows. After racing precariously over several slanted roofs and trying all the windows, I finally found one open and I startled the inhabitants of the flat as I slid in.

"The Gestapo is arresting people! Sorry for scaring you, but I leave through your door!" I shouted. I took three steps at a time down the stairway. Carefully, I peeked out through the gate and saw the Gestapo and Schutzpolitzei still busy a few houses away. Sweating all over and trying to appear calm, I slowly walked out and went in the opposite direction. They might have been taking prisoners in a revenge for some other violent happening, or they might have been looking for specific individuals. With the Gestapo it was the best practice not to find out, but simply to avoid.

My uncle did not have a telephone and I never had a chance to see him again. I never found out what the Gestapo was doing there that day. In August 1944, toward the end of the German occupation the entire Stare Miasto square was totally destroyed during the Warsaw Uprising.

No one ever knew what happened to my uncle.

* * *

Food became more scarce in the City of Warszawa. We had not eaten fresh meat for months. My parents decided to send me out to a friend's farm in the country where they still managed to raise a few cattle and some poultry. We hoped they would be able to sell us a little meat and fresh produce. There were no telephones, so no arrangements could have been made in advance. I was given a sum of money, good-luck wishes and lots of advice as I left for the train station.

Travel permits were not yet required as long as the destination was not near important military installations or a border. When I came to the Warszawa Central Railroad Station, it was full of rowdy German soldiers, their friends and families. Some soldiers were having a drink, others were giving their wives or girlfriends goodbye kisses. On the other hand the Polish travellers were unobtrusive. Old "babas" and mothers cried quietly and hugged their loved ones who were leaving.

I went to the wicket to get my ticket to a small village, a couple of hours train ride away. "Dziesiec zlotych, prosze," said the ticket seller. I handed him 10 zloty for a return ticket to the village.

There were scores of people like myself on the train-poorly dressed and hungry looking Polish men, women and children carrying every possible form of luggage. The train was packed. I was unlucky in finding a seat, so I stood in the aisle of a coach. It had several two bench cabins with sliding doors along the side.

We were just on the outskirts of the city when the train pulled to a stop at a small station.

"Alle Leute heraus," screamed a German commander. Several SS-men wearing their typical metal chest-plates and waving black machine guns, ordered everybody off the train. (SS stands for "Schutzstaffel", translated it means Protection Staff. Those were the people responsible for enforcing the rules of the Third Reich.) Lining all the passengers on the side of the platform, they began to check all the papers and belongings of all of us.

To my horror, I saw a young man, check to make sure the Germans were not watching, then jumping off the far side of the platform. He ran toward a nearby forest. He was clever and ran in a zigzag pattern. A soldier spotted him and shouted to the others. They all jumped forward, pushing the assembled people out of their way. The soldiers knelt down

for a better aim. A long series of submachinegun bullets were fired at the
fleeing man.

"What's the matter with you, Gustaf?," asked one soldier with a grin. I
was standing close to these Germans. I heard him talking to his colleague
who was kneeling beside him, swearing and desperately working his
Schmeiser which had jammed..

"Don't you remember how to kill a Polish swine?"

I hoped the escapee got away, but several of the guards went after
him, shouting and shooting.

This episode disrupted the search. The Germans already had a sizeable
pile of parcels taken from the travellers. The train lines were limited.
There were lots of troops to transport and, I am sure, scheduled deliveries
to be made. The Germans decided they could not hold up our train and
block the line any longer.

Of course, Germans were permitted to return to the train first. Next the
locals were ordered back on the train which, emitting lots of steam and
sounds, started on its way again. As we passed many towns and villages I
could see some ruins and burnt-out houses. Only the populated areas
showed any real destruction. All the foliage made the country side appear
unspoiled. As autumn approached it turned from green to yellow or red; it
looked lovely.

We arrived at my stop. The station was very small and the village had only a couple of streets. A few people and some horse drawn wagons were the only traffic. To my surprise, there were no Germans in sight at that moment.

I enjoyed my walk through the village which had not been bombed or shelled during the invasion. The sandy main street had been paved with round "kocie lby" cobblestones. My parents had given me directions to our friend's home. Nothing was committed to writing, because the Germans would not spare any effort to check all information in hope of coming across smuggling or anything illegal. They were known to jail anybody for any periods of time, or to simply shoot them on the spot.

I found the friend's home, to which we had come for vacation in the previous, more peaceful times. I knocked on the door and a nervous voice asked:

"Who is it?"

"This is Alex Jadach, I was here on vacation four years ago. Do you remember Mr. Jadach and his family spending a summer vacation with you?"

There was some whispering and moving around and the door slowly opened. Upon entering, I was surrounded by the typical country smell and the warm air from the burning stove.

"Please come in, we haven't seen you for such a long time. How's Mrs. Jadach these days?"

"Oh, all right. I guess. In the city everything is different than it is here," I added.

"Please sit down and take your coat off. Would you like a mug of warm milk?"

"Yes, thank you," I said "I haven't had such a treat for quite a while." I sat down on the bench beside the big table and stretched my legs.

"Yeh, it is sure a long time since you were here," said the farmer as he tried to roll a cigarette. "Want one?" He offered me the "bibulka", [cigarette paper] and a pouch of tobacco.

A long silence came upon us while he rolled and lit his smoke. I could hear the wood crackling in the stove.

Meanwhile, I looked around and saw that the room had not been painted for a long time. Before the war this family white washed the whole house inside and out. It usually killed the bugs and made the surroundings lighter and friendlier. The straw mattress on the big shelf behind the stove was still there. "It must still be the warmest place to spend the night," I thought. The big table and the two benches were as nice as I remembered and scrubbed clean as before. Holy pictures of the Saints, with traditional dried flowers tucked behind, still adorned the walls. A cat sat close to the warm stove licking its paw and face. Here, it was cosy and peaceful, unlike the city I had left.

"What happened to your regular white washing of the house?", I asked.

He took a while to answer.

"The Germans have confiscated many things. The town offices and agriculture warehouses have almost nothing left. You cannot buy lime anymore. We have large quotas of produce that must be delivered to the occupation authorities every fall. If we don't obey, they come and sentence us to hard labour or put us in prison. The inspector comes without warning to check produce storage areas. Our community has a flag warning system but he finds a victim every time."

I realized, as we slowly drank the boiled milk, that the country was not as untouched as I had thought . A fire crackled in the big stove and the kitchen was filled with a good aroma. The farmer's wife occasionaly stirred the black kettle on the stove with an enormous, wooden spoon. Outside, I could hear chickens cackling and some cattle lowing. That reminded me of my business.

"My mother told me to ask you if you could sell us any kind of meat? We haven't eaten meat for several months and would be great if we could buy some from you." He lifted his hat to the back of his head and started to slowly scratch his uncombed, sweaty hair. His wife continued to stir her kettle but I was sure she heard what I said. After a long silence the farmer said:

"We do not have very much ourselves, the inspection is so strict. But, I guess, because of our friendship, and for the Mighty Lord's good-will, we might be able to find something for you."

He got up and summoned his wife, they both went out to the court yard. I started to doze off; it had been an eventful morning. Before I knew it, I was almost asleep.

"Here, you can have this rooster," said the farmer standing in front of me. "The inspector missed him the last time," he added while lifting up the carcass, just killed and already plucked. He wrapped the bird in old newspapers and put it in a well used brown bag.

"Sorry, it is all we can spare. Times have changed and we too do not eat very well any more."

I handed him the money Mother had given to me. He did not want to accept but after some persuasion he took it and hid it under his shirt. He whispered something to the woman and she went to the attached shed and came back with a loaf of bread.

"You're so nice and you're starving. Here, take this. We don't have too much but we will share it with you. God bless you and your family." They rewrapped the parcel and tightened all the strings and paper layers to make it secure. I was treated to a bowl of delicious home made soup with some meat and lots of potatoes in it before I started my journey back to the city

We said goodbye and I walked back to the railroad station. I had not realized there would be so many people. Like myself, they were carrying all sizes, shapes and colors of parcels. Some parcels were wrapped in bed sheets or pillow covers. Some people were carrying old luggage reinforced with strings. After presenting my ticket and walking back and forth on the platform, I realized that most of some one hundred passengers waiting for the train to Warszawa had the same purpose as me. We were all bringing back food to the starving city.

The Germans knew perfectly well what was happening.

A patrol consisting of three SS-men marched down the platform shouting and waving their machine-guns and started taking people's belongings. My turn came quickly and I saw my dear chicken tossed on a big pile of parcels on the platform.

News came that the train was late. One of the three German guards watched the precious pile while the other two went in for a beer. The canteen was, of course, NUR FUR DEUTSCHE. We, Polish people, could not even peek inside without causing trouble for ourselves.

I was angry. What would my mother say? What would we eat? The farmer's family had not only deprived themselves but had taken a risk giving me food. I did not want the Germans to have it. Impulsively, I walked briskly towards the pile, not caring at that moment whether I was shot or shouted at. Luckily, the guard was looking the other way as I spotted my chicken. I could not resist. I grabbed my parcel and turned abruptly around. I walked very slowly to the other end of the platform, half-expecting a bullet in my back at any time.

We could see the train coming. It appeared to be full and when it stopped, very few passengers got off. Somehow we all managed to board it, with some people clinging to the outside. The trip back was overcrowded and uneventful. Everybody worried about another German search, so I got off at the outskirts of the city instead of taking the train to the downtown Main Station. I started the ten kilometer walk home with no intention of losing my precious chicken again.

Walking across the fields I met a boy I knew and he said to me:

"Did you hear about the Underground executing a German spy in this field?"

"No," I said. "When did it happen?"

"Last evening. The field was full of police and Gestapo this morning. They took his body away. Come, I'll show you the place."

We crossed the recently harvested grain field where the stubble still stood. There we spotted a pair of heavy brown frame glasses. I lifted them and threw them a way as quickly as I could. They were covered with blood of the dead man. All the way home I wondered what the man had done and how his treachery had been discovered.

"Oh I am so relieved you're back," exclaimed my mother. "We were so worried about you. How did it go?" I triumphantly opened my heavy jacket and proudly pulled out the parcel containing the chicken and the bread.

What a celebration we had!

Author, wearing Jurek dad's uniform posing in Jurek's apartment.

Chapter 8

FREEING OF PRISONERS

March 26, 1943

"Rudy" (a pseudonym of Jan Bytnar, one of the most active officers in the Underground), was arrested by the Germans.   As a result of a betrayal, at 4:30 a.m. the Germans raided his apartment, where they found a lot of incriminating material. In addition to "Rudy", the Gestapo arrested his father, but his sister was spared as she had not returned home that evening because of the curfew.

"Rudy," the commanding officer of the Underground platoon "South Section", was a remarkable young man. He was extremely involved in anti-German activities. As a commander, "Rudy" was very well liked. He encouraged his Scout-soldiers to feel hope for a free Poland. He was also known for his incredible "gadgets" which could start fires or blow up German installations. On an earlier occasion, "Rudy" managed to escape the Germans who had surrounded his apartment building. The Gestapo went from flat to flat checking papers and detaining a few people. Fortunately, the Germans forgot to secure the back of the building. "Rudy," not wanting to be questioned, attached a rope to the leg of a heavy dining room table and lowered himself down to the ground. He simply walked out of the cordoned area. But now they got him.

Immediately after "Rudy's" arrest an instant alarm was raised by the Underground Scout Movement. This alarm resulted in the notification of all involved parties to take action. Right away all the weapons and magazines were moved to new, secret locations.

At the Gestapo headquarters, "Rudy" was interrogated in the most brutal way. The Germans demanded names, addresses and information that would assist them in breaking the underground movement. According to the numerous stories told me right after the event, the many books (e.g. *Wrobel* by Bogdan Deczkowski) and films, the questionig tactics consisted of hitting him with a wood cudgel, kicking him with heavy boots and holding his face in a bucket of water. This torture did not give them the information they wanted. When this measure failed, the Gestapo tried to break him by torturing in front of him people he knew. When this did not bring any results, his physical torture was resumed. Again, he was beaten by three husky, weight-lifting types, Gestapo interrogators. When he was down they struck him with bats and a "pejcz", a heavy leather strap with a metal ball at the end. Every time he fainted, they kicked his stomach or his genitals.

"Rudy" was quickly reduced to an inhuman condition. He had been a healthy young man, of a rather small frame, but in excellent shape. His tortured body was blue and brown and beyond repair.

Every afternoon, after the interrogation sessions with the Gestapo, he was transported with other prisoners, back to the Pawiak, a Warszawa's fortress-like old jail. Some of the other prisoners tried to care for him. They were used to seeing tortured bodies but were shocked by the extent of the damage to "Rudy". Some sat by him through the night, changing wet rags, giving him water or washing off dried blood.

The Germans continued their interrogation and torture. Even when "Rudy" was on a stretcher, he did not tell them what they wanted to know. We all mourned our brave hero.

Our SAD-300 unit (later called, "Zoska Battalion") received the secret news of what was happening and made a suggestion to the higher command to free him. There was a debate on the importance of freeing "Rudy." People had different opinions about who was more important. Finally, plans were made and approved to attack the trucks moving the prisoners to the jail. Twice, the Underground soldiers were ready for action but our plans were foiled as the prison van had changed its route. However, the third time the plan was put into action.

I was heartsick at not being included in this important action; maybe my young age played against me. But from the accounts of my friends I know exactly what happened. Three attack groups of the Underground Force assembled on a busy down town street. They mingled, appearing to be part of the crowd. One group was equipped with pistols and grenades, another with gasoline bottles which would explode on impact, and the last one had a couple of machine guns. They were hidden in nearby ruins.

The commanding officer nervously watched the look-out, two blocks away, who stood in front of a big store display window, at the busy intersection. He was supposed to take his hat off and bow as a sign that the prisoner's van was approaching. The CO was nervous because the man had turned his back to the street and appeared to be interested in the contents of the store window instead of watching for the prison van. The

CO did not realize that the look-out could see the entire street reflected in the window.

Despite the prearranged signal of only bowing, the look-out turned, took his hat off and waved it frantically. The prison van was approaching. It was a French made truck, a Renault. At this moment, a Polish policeman in his familiar dark-blue uniform had unexpectedly appeared and crossed the street right in front of one of the groups.

"This is an action of the Polish Armed Forces. Hand me your gun," said one of our men drawing his pistol. The policeman did not believe him. He jumped back and tried to pull out his own weapon. "Zoska" tried to shoot the police officer in the legs but his pistol jammed. Someone else fired his gun wounding the cop.

The shot created panic among the pedestrians. People ran for protection. The driver of the prison van saw the commotion and instead of turning right, rapidly changed his direction to the left. But it was too late. Two gasoline bottles landed on the hood, resulting in fiery explosions. The flames engulfed the cab. The driver fell over the steering wheel and two Gestapo men jumped out with their black uniforms on fire.

Gunfire erupted all over. The second shot on the street did not come from the Gestapo but from the blue uniformed policeman. He supported the Germans to his last moment. The Underground's first fatal casualty was one of the machine gun operators who received a hit in the stomach from him. Another shot ended the treachery of the policeman. Bullets ricocheted from the stone walls of the old, historic Arsenal as one of the Polish sections attacked the German guards. The last German alive ran down an alley.

The cab of the truck and the engine burned without exploding The back canopy of the prison van opened and the prisoners jumped out so quickly they rolled on top of each other. Some stood in shocked disbelief, others asked for guns. "Rudy" was carried out of the burning truck. The injured were loaded into waiting cars. The CO's whistle announced the termination of the action. From one of the government buildings a long series of machine gun fire was directed at the Underground Forces. Since it was on the route of our escape, a group was dispatched to attack.

Another Pole, "Alek", was shot, but lying on the pavement just before he passed out, he threw a grenade into the German building. There was a big explosion and the firing stopped. The rescue force retreated quickly.

"Rudy" was in a happy mood and tried to smile at everyone. He was in terrible pain, and a few days later, despite receiving the best possible medical attention, he died. Alek died too. They were buried in the large Powazki Cemetery under false names. After the war, their bodies were exhumed and re-interred with proper honours in the section of the grounds reserved for the Zoska Battalion.

Chapter 9

THE GHETTO

Soon after the invasion, the Third Reich began its harassment of Warszawa Jews. I remember adults arguing about new German proclamations which restricted Jewish businesses and froze their bank accounts. I distinctly remember seeing many residents of the city wearing white arm bands with the blue Star of David.

Early in the war, many people in our part of town seemed to approve of the slow strangulation of the Jews. Others only professed support and some, like my mother, seemed bewildered.

"I've seen it before," she told me during a power outage one evening in the spring of 1940. "One set of people fixes blame on another. Then they don't have to answer for problems themselves."

She said it was wrong, but told me not to say anything publicly.

"When people with power start pointing fingers, Aleksander, it is always safest to stay out of view."

But she continued her visits to Mrs. Rosenstat and others. Mrs.Rosenstat was an old friend and a Jew, until the evening she came home and told "Tatus" that her friend was gone.

"Her apartment was requisitioned," she explained, "and her whole family has been sent to the ghetto; now all Jews have to live behind the walls."

The Germans had made all kinds of promises: talking about a Holy Land, a separate state, or repatriation to another country. Even Mrs. Rosenstat had been hopeful that things might be tolerable under the Nazis. But this new and total isolation of Warszawa Jews seemed threatening. The people of Poland began to realize how serious the situation was. Even factions in Poland who had been antisemitic before the war, were horrified at seeing the ghettos constructed in almost every town.

"I've read about it," said my father. "The Germans say the Jews will be safer in one place, and can continue living as a community. They, however, said so many things . . . ."

He only stared at his hands. The months had sapped him. He seemed so unsure now , weakened. I'd even heard him sobbing late at night.

By autumn of that year, we had all seen the walls of the Ghetto and one afternoon in mid-October, my friend Zbyszek suggested we go in. The idea seemed preposterous but Zbyszek said he knew people who were making good money smuggling things in and out of the Ghetto.

"And," he added with a smirk, "there are beautiful women who will do things for food."

We were reluctant to leave our relatively tranquil part of Warszawa but Zbyszek, who was older and considered a tough, convinced us by saying that, anyway, the underground was looking to establish contacts between the Ghetto and the outside. When he suggested we could make quite a reputation for ourselves by performing this mission, Antoni and I agreed to go with him.

The next morning, we took the tram downtown and approached the Ghetto at the Grzybowska Street. Labourers were adding to the wall, some mixing cement in a big flat pan, adding white caulk and using long-handled mixing oars. Others loaded buckets, swinging them onto their shoulders before carrying them to the stone masons.

We saw Wehrmacht guards talking with each other and not paying much attention to the comings and goings, although we soon realized that nobody with a blue and white armband passed through the gate.

We followed the wall for perhaps half an hour before noticing a tram passing through another gated entrance. The tram was nearly empty, but we were more interested in the fact that it did not stop for inspection. We had already decided that scaling the wall would be too dangerous, an obvious infraction.

Maybe, I suggested, we could just ride the tram in and play stupid if we were questioned. After all, we weren't really doing anything illegal, as far as we knew.

We backtracked and hopped the next tram, looking nervously at the Polish policeman who manned the other car. There were only five or six other passengers. We huddled in the car and talked excitedly as a way to explain how we had missed our stop. But nobody challenged us and we were soon within the walls.

We walked about aimlessly. As in the rest of Warszawa, there were many people on the street, more than downtown.. I noticed nobody of my age.

"Bah, I don't see any beautiful women," snorted Zbyszek as we rounded a corner. Then Antoni held out his arm to stop us. Down the street a hundred meters was an old man in rags, standing by a basket containing what looked like shrunken potatoes. Two German soldiers were taunting him, and one poked him with his rifle butt.

The old man fell to the ground and one of the soldiers kicked his basket, sending a half-dozen potatoes along the sidewalk. The soldiers pulled him to his feet and shouted something. The old man began a little dance, staring down in shame.

The two Germans laughed and pointed at the old Jew's feet, which were wrapped in old rags.

"Where are your dancing shoes now?" shouted one in Polish. After a few minutes, they clapped in mock applause and walked away, carefully stepping on each of the old man's potatoes.

After they left we approached the old man, who sat on the pavement. I gave him some money while Antoni retrieved his basket.

"You are not Jews," said the old man, looking up at me. We said we were not, and that we had only wanted to come and see.

"See the Jews dance?" he asked.

Others were gathering and I was feeling uncomfortable. Too loudly, Zbyszek said we were helping to fight the Nazis. A well-dressed man stepped forward and motioned for us to follow him.

"We can't," I whispered to Antoni. "What if he's Gestapo?"

"He would have shot us already," said Antoni.

We followed a very short distance to a small appartment down some steps. A girl about my age greeted us. She had hair and eyes as black as coal. I thought she was the most beautiful girl I had ever seen. The man said his name was Reuben and introduced her as his daughter, Rhona.

"You are mad to be here, absolutely crazy," he said. Zbyszek only stared at Rhona while the man continued.

"The conquerors seek to destroy us. They'll get you to help them. We are lost. First they take our dignity, then our livelihood, then our homes, then our lives. After us, it will be your turn. Murderers work like that."

Rhona brought us a weak tea as her father told of things he had seen. He told of beatings and random killings. He said he had seen Jews turn on each other. He told of a mother he had seen who had simply tossed her baby over the Ghetto wall.

"I tell you this because you have youth and - for now - freedom," he said. "Get away if you can but, in the name of God, do not ever again go walking into the line of fire."

I dared ask Rhona where she went to school.

"We have no schools any more," she answered softly. "We have nothing. Only each other."

I envied the look of love she gave her father.

"I want to help; what can I do?" I asked. "Let me get you out."

"There are too many of us," said her father. "Now, you better go."

At the door, Rhona's hand brushed mine and I blushed. Zbyszek elbowed me and winked but I could only look at her.

"Remember us," she said sadly as they closed the door.

* * *

I resolved to do more.

We walked out of the Ghetto, held up by a German soldier for identification and a pat-down at the gates.

"We were just visiting the Jew Zoo," said Antoni when the soldier asked what business we had in the ghetto. The German laughed and waved us on our way.

Eight days later, I wrapped some bread, sausage and a newspaper in a small package. Alone, I boarded the same tram which this time stopped at the Ghetto gate.

"What's that; where do you think you are going?" asked the Polish guard as he stood over me. I could smell garlic on his breath.

"My teacher asked me to deliver this to an old friend," I stammered.

He tore the package from my hands and tore the newspaper wrapping.

"No," he shouted. "That is illegal. A German guard would be taking names. You're lucky that today, I am the one, Polski. Get home and don't ever come back."

I tried again, on foot, at a different time four days later. The German at the gate routinely confiscated my meager parcel but he let me in with a smug smile.

"Many who go in come out in a hearse," he called after me. I could only think of Rhona, as I had almost constantly for two weeks. I almost ran to her apartment.

A large, bearded man in black opened the door only slightly after I had knocked for many minutes.

"No Reuben. No Rhona. They're gone," he said gruffly to my question. I could hear babies and the shuffle of many people in the appartment.

The man shut the door. I called through it.

"Go away," he shouted. "They're gone."

The same German soldier frisked me thoroughly as I walked out.

"Better you not come back," he said in German. "Smugglers - shot. Jew symphatizers - shot."

I never went into the Ghetto again. But I shall remember them. always.

The Germans herded about 450,000 Jewish people into the Warszawa Ghetto. By 1943, all but 56,000 had been sent to extermination camps.

In April of that year, the Warsaw Ghetto began fighting back, just to die with dignity. They stood no chance of winning even with the arms supplied by the Home Army and with the Underground's assistance. A few dozen people survived this final assault by escaping through sewer tunnels or hiding deep in secret basements. About 5000 people had escaped from the Ghetto before the 1943 Uprising. My Mother and I were involved in helping Jewish escapees, and my Mother was decorated, posthumously. Jewish friends placed on her grave a brass plaque in her honour at the Powazki Cemetery.

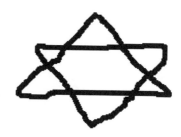

Chapter 10

THE ARSENAL AT ROZANA STREET

Underground action against the German occupation forces continued to increase. Despite severe reprisals for each act, the Underground grew braver. The Germans had escalated their campaign of control through terror, and were summarily executing merchants and other citizens for such petty violations as food smuggling and currency exchange. Their brutality seemed to knit Warszawa residents together against the new masters.

The Ghetto Uprising of spring, 1943, also set an example and served to galvanize resistance.

Jurek Horczak, age 17, and his 12-year-old cousin Tolek were two of the few contacts I had within the Polish Underground. I actually knew only four people, which for security reasons, was best.

Jurek, code name "Wrobel", and I were storing arms for the Underground (Home Army was its military arm) in his apartment. The apartment was chosen because only two youth lived there, thereby putting less people at risk. In addition to the weapons, we had also stashed forged papers, including a new ID for my "Tatus". We had half a dozen hand guns, a machine gun, some grenades and two boxes of pencil-like timing devices with a small, color-coded clip. They resembled ball-point pens. When activated, the color indicated the time remaining before it would burst into a small searing flame.

Under the cover of night, at appointed times we had been slipped these few precious arms by secretive messengers, men and women. The weapons had been recovered from the sporadic parachute drops that marked the Allied efforts to bolster the Polish Underground, in particular in Warszawa. We were told that the high casualty rate of planes making the long flight from Great Britain to Poland made the Allied Forces unable to provide more concerted assistance.

I remember vividly that evening of August the 4th, 1943, when the summer warmth coaxed my parents and me out of our flat. We sat silently in the courtyard on Narbutta Street, listening to the distant murmur of voices. People sat in their backyards enjoying the warm evening and a few precious peaceful moments. By a German edict, electricity was cut off at night and it seemed as if the entire population had ventured out to absorb what might be the last natural warmth of the year.

There was little conversation in our group. I sat considering the delicious prospect of blowing up a Nazi "buda" (a military troop transport truck covered with a tarpaulin). I even dared fantasize about watching a bridge topple with the force of a device that I, Aleksander Jadach, had handled in our little arsenal.

At times, Warszawa was bombed nightly by the Russians. It was in those days that I began to distinguish the different sounds of the falling bombs. German bombs whistled. Russian bombs sounded like big trees swaying in a strong wind. Later, I would come to know British and American ordnance. British bombs fell silently while American ones produced gurgling sound, like a bottle of soda being slurped.

Suddenly, that night, came a loud explosion from a distance. There was no warning, no wailing sirens announcing a Russian air raid.

The voices around us stopped. Every building, fence and tree seemed to be listening. There came another blast and some very subdued machine gun fire; then a third explosion.

My father, who used to speak in sharp emphatic style, spoke with the mumble that we were now becoming used to.

"Russians," he nodded to the darkening sky. "And with such an efficiency they are bombing the poor Poland."

He wiped a tear while pretending to scratch his chin. He stared at the ground, permanently embarrassed by his small part in the "medieval" Polish army that the Nazis had broken quickly almost like thin glass.

I wanted to give him strength. I almost blurted out my faith in the cashe of arms secreted on Rozana Street. Then I realized that my "Tatus" must not know such things. He, after all, was the ruined past while Jurek, I, and the Underground - we were the brave future.

The city felt silent again. Then we heard softly running feet. Two figures appeared in the darkness of the night and quickly clambered over the wire fence. Jurek and Tolek were standing in front of us.

There were several people within earshot and we knew that one of the families were Volksdeutche, new German settlers with some understanding of Polish. They were committed to winning Nazi favour by reporting anything unusual, so we automatically avoided creating a stir. "Tatus" rose and announced that the curfew was in effect and we should go into the house.

"For heaven's sake, what happened?" I asked. "What are you doing here at this hour? You know you will be shot on sight after curfew!" I looked down in the very dim light of the candle and saw that he was barefoot and his feet were bleeding. Something dreadful must have happened. Jurek owned his father's Polish Officer boots made of soft, black leather. He was very proud of them and wore them at all times. He kept them in good shape.

Now my mother brought a cloth soaked in warm water to care for his cut feet. The boys sat down still breathing heavily. "Tatus" checked the covers of the windows making sure that no light was getting out. It took Jurek a while to catch his breath and answer

"We ran all the way from our place," he said. "It started when we heard a "buda" some distance away, coming closer and closer. I realized the Nazis were searching door to door. I could see them from the window. There was an SS with a machine gun, a Polish policeman, and a civilian - probably a Gestapo. And soldiers, a few of them. Every couple of minutes they would drag someone to the truck. They'd swear and beat them. People, half dressed men or women, were screaming and crying. They came closer and Tolek started crying. I didn't know what to do."

"But you are a child, with nothing to hide," said my father softly.

"No," answered Jurek, looking up and right and my "Tatus". "I'm Home Army, a fighter. We had arms hidden in our apartment. Lots of them."

My father looked at the window while Jurek continued his tale: he had pulled the Czechoslovakian machine gun from the closet, loaded it and set it up on its stand pointing towards the door. He had then picked out the Browning 7.65 mm pistol and asked Tolek if he also would like a gun. "They weren't going to get us; not without a battle. I wasn't going to let them just take it all," Jurek said firmly.

My mother had now quietly finished tending his bruised feet and she brought a pair of my socks as Jurek continued: "I could hear them at the next door. I put down two 'Filipinkas' from our supply hidden in the cupboard, one by the window and one by the door. We weren't going to go quietly like my parents had."

I knew well those home-made "Filipinka" canister bombs. They were similar to regular grenades but exploded on impact. They had no timing devices, just a touch and they blew up. With one kilogram of explosives they were very powerful and very dangerous.

"Then," Jurek said, "they pounded at the door. I'd cleverly used a little child's voice, saying that I wasn't allowed to open because I was alone. They had said they were there to help, and it was alright to let them in."

That was when Jurek had flung the door open. He had caught a glimpse of a relaxed SS soldier in green uniform with a machine gun pointed down. The Gestapo fellow stood beside dressed in his civilian coat and hat, both hands in the pockets. Jurek said he thought they were both smiling. The Polish policeman was on the way up the stairway.

"I just fired away. I shot dead the bloody bastards," he told us. "They were falling over each other."

Then he had slammed the door, run to the living room window and tossed a "Filipinka" at the German "buda." Just before it exploded he saw two soldiers, who moments earlier were standing and chatting, frantically getting their submachine guns off their shoulders.

"What a sound," he now said, his eyes sparkling. "The explosion was horrendous, the glass shattered and fell from all the windows. The two soldiers just disappeared . . . disintergrated."

It was all so fast. The truck was on fire. Next, Jurek had returned to the front door, opened it and tossed another bomb, the force of which had blown his door off its hinges.

"Then, I could hear from the backyard, where there was an entrance to the building, a guard shouting:

"Heinz, wo bist du?" [Heinz-where are you?] and I could hear his footsteps as he came into the building. Grabbing a third "Filipinka," I opened the other window and jumping out ran around the corner of the house. Again, I threw the bomb into the staircase entrance and jumped backwards. After the explosion there was total stillness broken only by Tolek's sobbing and the sound of a few pieces of glass settling around us. All was quiet on the street but in the distance I heard an air alarm. I pulled Tolek from behind the sofa-bed, told him to be quiet, and we left. Everything happened so quickly that I didn't get my high officer's boots that had belonged to my Dad and I loved so much," he whispered, looking sadly at his bandaged feet.

Our room was quiet. We had listened to his story in appalled silence. I, more than my parents, realized the immediate grim consequences of the disaster.

"We must leave this district right away," said Jurek. Then he said to my "Tatus":

"Your picture was in my apartment ready for insertion in a set of forged papers." My father looked ashen.

"I was in on it. I am in on it. They'll know about me," I said. "And about you too, father."

He sat perplexed, looking at the floor.

"We have to run. Fast," I implored.

Jurek jumped up from his chair and grabbed my wrist.

"Yes, we've got to run," he repeated.

"Not me," said my "Tatus". "I'm not active, I'm only with the reserves. The Germans have no fight with me. I am old and of no threat to them. But yes, you must run. Fast and far."

He thrust some bills in my pocket and kissed my cheek. Moments later we were at the door.

Mother was listening, her arms were suddenly wrapped around me as she sobbed quietly. Dad only stared at the framed family pictures, barely visible on the wall in the flickering light of the candle.

"Don't say where you're going, we must not know. God bless you all," he said as we left.

These were the last words I ever heard from him and the last time I saw my "Tatus." He was arrested shortly after we escaped and sent to the Buchenwald concentration camp where, a year later, he died as a result of malnutrition, exhaustion and torture.

We stuffed pieces of bread in our pockets and within minutes we sneaked out. We walked and ran through a dark city. We were turned away by some people we knew and slept lightly on a carpet of pine needles in a park. Toward the morning, we approached the home of Jacek Karpinski, who welcomed us with open arms.

We were later told that the Germans, expecting heavy resistance, took an entire battalion back to Jurek's place. Some prisoners, Germans, and tenants had died in the first blasts, but some prisoners had escaped and most of Jurek's neighbours had fled. The British-made sabotage gadgets and arms found in Jurek's apartment made the Germans put up posters and offer a large reward for our capture. They identified Jurek, little Tolek, and me as wanted criminals. Later that year, Jurek was captured by a "tajniak", an undercover Gestapo agent. He was spotted by his new pair of Polish officer boots - his fatal love. He was tortured at the Szucha Alle in the Gestapo headquarters. He later died, nobody knowing how and where. The valiant unsung hero of the Underground, posthumously decorated with the highest Polish military decoration for bravery - *Virtuti Militari Cross*. Tolek survived the war as a much decorated soldier.

Chapter 11

THE ATTACK ON THE BORDER STATION IN SIECZYCHY

A major offensive by several cells of the underground Home Army against border stations between the Generalgouvernement (as central Poland was now called by the Germans) and German occupied Russia was initiated. In the late summer of 1943, border stations were to be destroyed and weapons and war materials taken for the Underground.

It was August 1943 when the order came through the underground channels that we should prepare to liquidate a German border station east of Warszawa. The operation was disguised as a school class trip to study the forests. It took place on the 20th.

Our underground cell members were told to meet two or three together at different points in the city. The small groups were to congregate at a specific location in a forest outside a nearby village. To avoid creating suspicion, I travelled with a school buddy. Everyone was to arrive by different means. Carrying our shoulder bags with biology books and specimen jars in case we were stopped by a German patrol, we travelled by tram to the edge of the city. We caught a local train to the village and then we walked to our destination. We reached a small woodland clearing in the forest. Large trees surrounded us, birds were singing and the foliage had the beautiful color and smell of the early fall. The scene did not reflect our grim purpose.

As we walked through the forest, a man wearing civilian clothes approached us and said:

"Hi guys, are you here for the class?

We didn't know him, so we were very careful and confused. He might have been a German. We were just about to tell him a lie when our Group Commander appeared, greeted the civilian by name, and told us to stay quiet. We were ordered to lie down and be still. People continued to arrive and they were given the same order. After a while the bushes were full, but still. Underneath, the ground was alive with excitement.

To our horror, a big German Daimler car with German licence plates and swastika markings unexpectedly appeared. I thought our manoeuvre had been discovered and we would be shot. I was wrong. The young man driving this vehicle and wearing a German Nazi uniform with a big, red arm band and black swastika, spoke fluent Polish and was a member of the Polish Underground. He was the one who brought us guns, ammunition and explosives. He was the delivery man.

We were being assigned for our warfare weapons when a sudden signal from the posted lookouts sent us scrambling into the bushes again. After a few tense moments, one of our leaders, an officer wearing civilian clothes, stuck a handgun in his belt and motioned for me to get up. I followed him. Walking towards us was "Pan lesniczy", a local forest warden who carried a shotgun. This was normal, even under the German rule, as his job was to watch for poachers or peasants who would try to pick mushrooms or unlawfully gather wood.

He wore an unusual hat. It was a combination of a Tyrolean hat with a feather stuck in it and an American cowboy hat. This was his uniform, proof of his authority to patrol that section of the woods. He worked for the owners, who were under close German supervision.

We walked toward him quite casually and my companion and I were talking about the different vegetation and their biological names. The warden stepped towards us asking,

"What are you two doing in my woods?"

"Oh, nothing special, we are just on a biology class tour."

"You mean there are more of you out here?," he added with a tone of disbelief.

My commanding officer looked to me. I turned to the man and said:

"The whole class is here, is there anything wrong with that?"

"No, no," said the warden hastily, "but it is most unusual to have a group here so close to the Russian border."

"Well, come and meet my students," said the commander with his most charming smile. He was Tadeusz Zawadzki whose pseudonym was "Zoska," the same who five months earlier had commanded a platoon during the action at the Arsenal to free "Rudy."

"Yes, I would like to," answered the warden and walked briskly ahead of us. As soon as we reached the clearing, "Zoska" drew his gun while several guys jumped out pointing their weapons at the poor fellow. The warden dropped his double barrelled shotgun and slowly, with an expression of utter horror, raised his arms.

We could not take any chances with so many people and so much equipment involved in the operation. We took the warden with us to be sure he did not notify the authorities. He was handcuffed to a large boy whose orders were to control him.

Most of the fifty of us got rifles but some had Sten submachine guns or pistols. "Filipinka" hand bombs were also a main weapon. They were bigger then grenades and much more powerful. We were instructed to form a single file and follow each other through the woods and fields, avoiding populated areas. We were walking quietly, but from time to time somebody would step on someone's toes or get bumped by the butt of a rifle and a subdued swearing followed each episode.

As I marched, I was dreaming about my past. Dreams make you forget the reality and make you relax a little. My dreams were important in helping me survive.

One summer before the war and before I became the proud owner of a two wheel bicycle. I was driven around by the older boys and they took sharp turns, slanting the bicycle and causing my hair to stand up. The balloon tires bit into the sidewalk and the pavement. What a thrill of speed. I could hardly wait until I received my own bike.

Every day I walked to my school which was located a few blocks away. I knew every stone, every gate and window, every flower and tree on that fifteen minute journey. There were squirrels and birds which were special to me and which I named and kept feeding.

My friends and I had secret places to hide notes written in code words as part of our play. We had many exciting things to do. There was a school drama club and every Christmas time we performed on stage. We portrayed different people or animals, dressed in costumes which our mothers had made. There were displays of our projects and writings of poems. (Wacek Wilk-Wilczynski, one of our classmates, later became a well-known Polish poet. He is now living in Kielce, Poland.)

We all had little books with hard-covers, like the diaries of today's children. In those times, only best friends were allowed to write a poem to each other and draw or paint a small picture in these diaries. My friends always asked me to draw a scene of a jumping lion, since they considered me to be the class artist. These were precious treasures which we hid from our parents, or so we thought. We planned to keep them forever. In the course of my life, which has changed dramatically at least nine times, I lost nearly everything. Nothing remains from my childhood except a couple of pictures from the prewar period.

A terse command interrupted my reminiscing.

"Tshhh, be quiet, for Christ sake, keep your mouths shut," whispered "Zoska". As the night became darker we realized that our leaders were very familiar with the route.

The sour smell of the sweat of fifty marching men blended with the scent of pine forests. A persistent thought occupied my mind. How could a person have a Nazi uniform and a Nazi car? How could he operate without being caught and executed by one side or the other? My questions went unanswered.

We had marched for hours and I became very thirsty. I did not have anything to drink, but I had a piece of bread. I ate the soft part of the heel (European breads are harder) of the loaf, thus forming a cup. In the darkness of the night, as we were wading through a stream, I quickly bent down to scoop my bread cup full of water.

What an awful shock! My thirsty mouth filled with water full of horse manure. In my haste to quench my thirst I had already swallowed some of the foul water. I wanted to throw up, but I could not stop or step to the side. I could barely see the outline of the man in front of me and had to follow closely. I suffered in silence because it was not safe to talk or make any noise.

As we marched my mind again slipped back to my childhood.

I was thinking about something that happened to me when I was learning to skate. In those days there were small ponds a few blocks away from our house. In the winter my "Tatus" took me skating there. I was not very good, but with lots of time to practice I got better. What a pleasant feeling it was to learn to glide on the slippery surface.

One day "Tatus" left me at the pond skating while he went to buy cigarettes. A big boy approached me and, being friendly, I moved towards him. He quickly looked around and grabbed my beautiful new leather pilot hat with ear flaps. He jerked it off my head. With my hat firmly in his hand, he started to run away. I saw him running in my "Tatus" direction. I started to shout:

"Tatus, Tatus!" pointing my arms at the boy. The kid was clever, he instantly changed his direction and disappeared behind some buildings. My "Tatus" was cross. I did not blame him, but I could not blame the boy either. He probably came from a poor family and, rather than attending school, he was forced to meet ends, one way or another.

I remember I was angry but concerned for the boy.

I faded back to reality as we approached the village of Sieczychy shortly before midnight. We had to move around very quietly to avoid disturbing the village dogs. It was a beautiful night, with a bright moon making it easier to see. Ahead of us was a small hill which would give us some protection to launch our attack. Over the hill were the barracks containing a detachment of German soldiers guarding the border between the German and Soviet Union occupied sectors of Poland.

Orders were passed along in whispers from man to man. The youngest and least experienced were told to lie down between the trees, form a line and wait for the signal to open fire. My small group was used as a backup. The patrols soon returned reporting that there were about a dozen Germans. They were all sleeping except for the watchman, who moved around on the porch of the wooden barracks.

There was a quick glint of a torch signal. Somebody at the front tossed a "Filipinka." It landed short of the target and hit the gate on a small fence. A terrible explosion shattered the stillness of the night. The Germans seemed stunned. Nobody moved and nothing happened for a few seconds. Then the hell broke loose!

The loud command to attack came and we could hear a group running and shooting.

The assault ended quickly. All the Germans were dead and our people were in control. We had orders to come in and remove weapons and ammunition and load them on a wagon. We were told to search the bodies of the soldiers for weapons or valuables. A fat German lay dead just beside a bush. I bent down and from his pants pocket I pulled a silver pocket watch. It was attached by a chain and in the darkness I could not disconnect it, so it stayed behind. I walked away. I did not like this type of job. The guy was still warm. He was living just minutes ago but had to die in a foreign country for what? It did not make sense.

We apparently had one casualty, but a crushing one. We realized with horror that "Zoska" was dead! The fine young man, who had been so brave, was our only casualty of the operation. "He was shot by the German watchman as he led the attack," said one of our soldiers. "He was hit in the chest and died instantly." "Zoska's" body was loaded onto the wagon. The horse wagon had been requisitioned from the village for the transportation of the anticipated booty, and now the ammunition and weapons from the border station were piled around "Zoska's" body.

The journey home started. A patrol went ahead and my group formed the back troop. The farmer driving his wagon was in the middle. Our group commander took out a "Filipinka" and placed it on the road. Carefully, he removed the handle and piled some leaves around it. The one kilogram of explosives was ready: the slightest move would cause it to blow up with a tremendous explosion. The bomb was meant to delay any pursusing German forces. We hoped the villagers would not be the ones to disturb it.

After a long march, as the dawn was approaching, we reached the clearing in the woods where our car with German markings was parked. The body and the weapons were loaded. We were told to return to our homes in small groups. My friend Zbyszek Rudzisz and I went to the station to take the train back to Warszawa. The night was over but the memories of it would have haunted me for years.

Chapter 12

THE "PONURY" PARTISANS

Since the German raid at Rozana Street had incriminated me, I was now being hunted by the Gestapo and my presence in Warszawa became a risk both to myself and the people who were sheltering me. The time had come for me to leave the capital.

In the early fall of 1943, carrying my newly forged identity papers for the name "Marian Chmielowicz" and a few personal items, I left Warszawa. My school friend, Zbyszek Rudzisz, pseudonym "Audaniec," travelled with me. We had to pay a small bribe to travel without authorization, and boarded a steam locomotive heading south towards the Swietokrzyskie Mountains. Partisan units, commanded by Major Jan Piwnik, code name "Ponury," were operating there. Major "Ponury", trained in Great Britain by SOE, had been parachuted into Poland from a Polish RAF aircraft.

At a small village we left the train, walked through the settlement and into one of Poland's many, beautiful forests.

"Stoj bo strzelam!" [Stop, or I shoot!] came a command. "Jakie haslo?" [What's the password?].

You stop immediately when faced with the possiblility of a shot through your body. How do you muster a pass word when you do not know it?

We raised our hands. A guard, appeared from the bush and gave a short whistle. Two other men came from behind. After making a quick search for weapons, they guided us into the thicket.

A totally new world opened in front of our eyes. There they had a cosy camp with a few tents and some bonfires burning. People were sitting around or sleeping. I saw many different uniforms. People had German helmets to which they had tried to paint the Polish insignia, or a red and white band to represent the Polish flag colors. Most of them wore red and white bands on their arms.

We were taken to an officer with tremendously heavy eyebrows, who was carrying a large pistol and a grenade on his belt.

"What's your name?" he asked.

"Aleksander Marian Jadach, Sir"

"And you?" he looked at Zbyszek.

"Zbigniew Rudzisz, Major," he answered standing at attention.

"Where do you boys come from?"

"We are students from Warszawa," we both answered simultaneously. Briefly we reported to him our adventures over the past few months.

Fortunately, he decided to trust us. He recognized in us two 17-year-old Polish youths willing to put their lives on the line in fighting for the freedom of their country. Zbyszek and I were given some heavy soup and a big piece of country baked black bread. The food tasted smoky but very good in the fresh air. It was cooked in a large, 100 litre metal milk can hanging over an open fire. We were then told to rest on some blankets by one of the tents.

Zbyszek and I were very good friends but we had different personalities and points of view. We began to argue and as the hours passed by our voices got louder.

Finally, one of the officers came by and handed each of us a rifle, a German Mauser carbine. He directed us to a certain spot in the bush and told us to stand guard. We were ordered to take turns, ten minutes at a time. The gun had to be over our shoulder and we had to stand at full attention, no talking, no moving.

This incident taught us a lesson. After a few hours we were so tired that when we were finally dismissed we went straight to bed in the assigned tent. I drifted to sleep thinking about my father's stamp collection. In my early childhood, my "Tatus" occasionally would call me to his study and show me his collection. Little by little, I learned how to lift stamps up carefully with a pair of pincers and how to view them through a magnifying glass. I also learned what to look for in a stamp. The stamps were bathed in a bowl of warm water and dried between the sheets of thick blotting paper. Blotting paper was used in those days because everybody had pens with nibs dipped in ink. Gradually, I took over his magnificent stamp collection. I began looking for new, rare, species. What a peaceful hobby I had inherited from my "Tatus". Dreaming about our stamps I slowly drifted away.

At daybreak, there was a quiet parade. We all lined up, attendance was taken and reports were given. The group commanders reported to the battalion heads and they in turn to the next in command who finally reported to the CO himself, the famous Major Jan Piwnik - "Ponury."

"We are now going to march quietly for a few days, avoiding open spaces and villages, absolute silence is a must," Major "Ponury" said giving the two of us a long look. "Our mission is to meet up with a large gathering of all the Resistance Forces from the surrounding districts. Our 1944 strategy against the German occupying forces will be planned."

After a quick breakfast, vigorous activity began all over the camp. Tents were taken down, weapons assembled and everything was made ready for travel. Fires were extinguished and covered over. All signs of the presence of seventy people were camouflaged in the best possible manner.

Shortly before 9 o'clock we started to move out in single file, forming a long column with a patrol in front and rear.

Zbyszek and I were assigned to "Komar" who was carrying an MG-42, a beautiful German machine gun weighing about 26 lbs. "Komar" was a good looking young man who always spoke positively. He must have been very well educated because he could discuss practically any subject in the world. He often talked about returning to his studies and reuniting with his young wife when the war was over.

Zbyszek and I were told to assist in carrying a stand made of two birch branches tied together. The front of the gun rested on it during the shooting. A steel box containing the ammunition belt was the other item we carried. This box was heavy, so Zbyszek and I changed the task every hour. Wrist watches were luxuries in those days, so we were very fortunate to have two in our company.

The first day passed uneventfully, no signs of people, villages or Germans. In the evening a new camp was erected in thick brush. Sentries were sent in all directions to guard the sleeping partisans.

Early next morning, after line-up, a two-wheel, horse-drawn wagon appeared, loaded with Stenguns. After a while it pulled away driven by two people, a young fellow and a female soldier. My curiosity was answered when somebody explained to me that these were locally and secretly produced 9 MM machine pistols called Stenguns which had to be tested before being distributed to the troops. After a few minutes, we heard a series of explosions and short bursts of machinegun fire. They were using a ravine to do their checking and after half an hour the wagon was back and we all started to march again. It was explained to me that the noise of the shooting might have attracted some unwanted attention so it was always best to leave the testing area quickly.

Our troops were now on a narrow path in another forest. The wagon had difficulty negotiating this path. Suddenly a signal came from the patrol ahead. We all took cover in the shrubs. Peacefully walking along the path was a single man who, I could have sworn, was talking to himself. Immediately he was stopped by our commanders and taken off for questioning. The front patrol did not wear any insignia which was safer in case of a sudden confrontation with the enemy. Some of the men wore German helmets, which would provide a few vital minutes of confusion if we ran into any real Germans.

Now this man thought we were Germans, and began to brag about all the people he had reported to the German authorities. A halt was called so a small detachment could go to the local village to check his story. We were laying around in the bushes enjoying the unexpected rest.

"Yes," came the answer; the man was a hated German collaborator who had caused a lot of suffering and grief to the local population.

There was no time during the war for court proceedings. A couple of men took him for a walk and we heard two shots. They returned alone.

After all this delay the column was formed again and we continued our march.

In the evening we found a little clearing and pitched our tents. The wagon full of machine guns was left in one of the villages we had passed.

My arms were sore from carrying the ammunition box. Zbyszek always "forgot" his turn to carry it and my hours became longer and longer. The stand he most often carried was light.

At one point, "Komar" had asked me to carry his machine gun. It was long and awkward but it seemed lighter than the ammunition belts in the bloody steel box. Sometimes it got entangled in low hanging tree branches.

That evening we took apart our guns and cleaned and oiled them. I had been assigned an old rifle with a clip of seven rounds. It was a single shot, hand repeated gun. It did not take me long to clean my weapon. After I had put it together again, I walked to the spread blanket on which "Komar" had taken his Maschinengewehr Mod. 42 apart. It was a fascinating piece of equipment and the only machine gun our small unit of seventy men had. Each part was thoroughly wiped and oiled again. I watched it with great attention.

"Olek, have you finished cleaning your rifle already?" came the clear, quiet voice of our group commander, who used my pseudonym in addressing me.

"Yes Sir," I answered promptly and walked over to show it to him.
"Where did you learn to service weapons?" he asked.

"In Warszawa. We had several basic courses on weapons. This is a very simple piece of equipment. This sort of Mauser carbine has served armies around the world for the past few dozen years." He started to talk, so I missed seeing the reassambling of the MG-42. They apparently got it during an attack on a small German outpost somewhere in the mountains. It served us well, being not too heavy and very fast shooting.

Late the next day, we arrived at our destination in steep, wooded hills. We met many other partisan groups. By the time we set up camp it was getting dark. It was not until the next morning that I was able to walk around and observe all the different units and their activities. Some were in black uniforms, others in green and still others in civilian clothes. We had one thing in common, however, we all wore the popular red and white armbands which distinguished us from the Germans. The small camps were spread over quite large area, fires were burning here and there and people slept or did their chores.

Later in the morning of that unforgettable October 28th, Zbyszek and I were summoned by the commander and ordered to join a patrol of seven to the local village. Instead of my regular rifle, I was equipped with a Stengun. We walked through the forest for a while, passing sentries hidden in the bush and exchanging the day's password.

The forest ended and in the distance we saw a small village. Somebody pointed to a house where a big, white sheet hung on the clothline. This was our signal that the village was free of Germans and we could enter safely. However, our commander was cautious. Another young fellow and I were sent ahead to explore and make sure that the area was "clean." We walked normally covering our Stenguns with our jackets. From a distance we would look like a couple of young men going to work.

The village houses all had straw roofs. There was no electricity or paved roads. Every home had its own, old fashioned well, with a bucket attached to a long pole hanging from another one balanced in the middle on a short axis suspended across two large poles. In those days this was a common sight at most of the village homes.

No alarm was raised as we entered the village so we signalled to the rest of the guys. Together we went to meet the Soltys (the local Mayor).

The Mayor's house looked a little larger then the others. We entered a big room which served as the kitchen and sleeping quarters. The Mayor was not entirely pleased when we presented him with an official blanket requisition order pre-authorized by the Polish Government-in-Exile, somewhere in England. We ordered him to give us a bull for food, meat needed for the troops in the hills. He did not have much choice when faced with guns and a requisition so he ordered somebody to summon a farmer with a bull.

What was brought to us was the biggest bull I had ever seen. It was rusty red and beautiful. Two of our guys grabbed the rope and started to lead the beast towards the forest. The farmer's wife arrived pulling her hair and lamenting loudly.

"Who is going to pay us back for our most precious possession? The bull is our life support. This piece of paper you're giving me isn't even good enough to wipe my ass with," she shouted.

"Be quiet, woman," snapped our commander in a harsh voice. "You will get paid when the war is over. Meanwhile this animal will feed hundreds of hungry soldiers, who are defending you from the bloody Germans. If we don't take it, 'Szkopy' [Krauts] will take it anyway."

He ordered us to turn and follow the two men and the bull in to the woods. We started to jog, only slowing down when we were among the first trees. It always felt safer when camouflaged by foliage.

"Psst," whispered the guy behind me. We were the last two in our small detachment.

"You know what the superstition is, don't you?" he asked in a subdued voice.

I told him I didn't.

"Every time we take a red bull it brings bad luck. You'll see, it always comes true," he explained.

We marched the rest of the way silently. At the camp, many people gathered around to admire the bull. Now, I could clearly hear people saying the same thing "Red bull - bad luck... red bull - no good."

The animal was shot, the carcass dressed. Water was boiling in several large metal milk cans. Vegetables and potatoes were added, garlic, salt and pepper. Pieces of meat were thrown into the cans or fried on sticks over the large bonfire. The kitchen tents were well organized to feed several hundred people.

The camp was full of activity and commotion. In one tent with the side totally open, a man vigorously pedaled a stationary bike which ran an electric dynamo. This produced power which in turn ran a radio transmitter. A man, was talking to somebody on that radio. He was wearing a striking, blue Royal Air Force uniform and speaking English, which, at that time, I did not understand. I was spell bound. It looked to me like there were enough armed forces here to end the war tomorrow.

I sat down for a rest, and began thinking about all the supplies gathered at our camp in the woods. My mind went back in time, recollecting a particular episode about supplies, this one being coal.

As a youngster, I was sitting in the wide window sill in our apartment in Warszawa watching the coal men. They brought a horse drawn wagon loaded with black, shiny coal. The horses struggled forward to pull the heavy load. We lived on the second floor so I had a good view of the scene below me. Mother went downstairs to count the number of big woven baskets the men carried on their shoulders to the basement. I asked "Tatus:"

"Why do they always bring some coal back to the wagon coming up from the basement?" Mom could not see, standing downstairs at the gate, that the men were removing coal.

My father ran down and shouted and the coalmen shouted back. I do not think they ever tried to steal coal from us again.

The aromas from the kitchen tents drifted my way to bring me back to reality in the partisan woods. We were getting mighty hungry and looking forward to a great meal when the spell was broken by abrupt, subdued voices.

"Red Alert! Red Alert! Germans are approaching with air and ground forces." Someone must have reported the great concentration of the Home Army. Frantically tents were taken down, personal belongings packed and weapons put in order.

"Komar," standing beside me had his personal Stengun over his shoulder. The Stengun was a primitive and very dangerous weapon, working by recoil. There was no safety on it. When cocked for the first shot and the trigger pulled, the explosion of the bullet moved the flying piece backward thus ejecting the empty shell and on the way back, automatically loading a new cartridge into the chamber, thus firing it. "Komar" was bending down to do the final wrapping on his backpack when his Stengun gently slid off his shoulder and the butt hit the ground.

Bang! The very loud shot just a few inches from me scared the hell out of me. I looked over and there was "Komar" lying on his back making funny movements, waving and jerking his arms and legs rapidly. At first, the people around us did not realize what was happening. In horror, we saw the little hole just above his ear where blood streamed in a pulsating motion bringing out gray pieces of his brain. The bullet had entered through his eye and out on the side. "Komar" died momentarily and his body was still.

Our Lieutenant came running, revolver in hand and shouted:

"What happened? Who did this? What's going on here?" After my brief explanation he barked a command to one of his subordinates: "Search 'Komar's' body! Remove everything! Don't leave anything. The personal papers, souvenirs, watch and money and above all photographs must be taken. And, of course, don't do the same stupid thing with your Stengun, understand?!"

"Hurry up! The rest of you form a marching column on the double. Follow me! The SS are on the attack!"

He had not finished speaking and in the sky above the trees we could see a couple of German Stukas dive bombers with their sirens on. They used this tactic to scare horses. They were dropping bombs just a few hundred yards from us. Trees and earth were flying up in the air, the ground was shaking. Our group had not been sighted, they were aiming at a group in black uniforms. These soldiers were carrying large white sheets, bulging with their belongings, strapped to their backs. They were very visible from the air. What a set-up.

We ran in line, single file. We were well camouflaged.

As we passed the kitchen tents the soup was still cooking and spreading a lovely aroma. I stumbled over something. It was the biggest country baked bread I had ever seen, almost the size of a wagon wheel. Since it was my turn to carry the light stand I managed to grab the precious bread and kept running, all the while trying to stay in line. Passing another kitchen tent, I saw a string of sausages in a big, open jute bag. I grabbed it too because I was mighty hungry. There were quite a few sausages on the string.

My happiness, however, was short lived. Bullets started to whine between the trees, ricochet and we began to run faster.

Suddenly, the string of sausages I was trying to stuff into my little side bag became lighter. With a quick glance, I saw that I was only holding

half of a small sausage in my hand, the rest were gone. Risking a fall, I turned my head to look back. I saw every man running behind me step right on those delicious things.

The bullets were whistling more often and closer to our heads. We tried to move even faster.

"Company stop, form a line on the top of the ridge to your right, six to ten feet spacing between you. Keep your heads low. The Germans are just approaching. Do not open the fire without my orders!"

We executed the command as quickly as possible. Another man had the machine gun and we followed him to a little depression. Lying down and loading our guns took just a few seconds.

We were calm despite the uproar. While there were lots of explosions and shots around us, we did not respond. The Stuka planes were gone, probably to reload their weapons or fill up on gas. Between the trees ahead of us we could now see some reflections, probably from the German infantry arms or their metal Schutzpolitzei breast plates. They were coming closer and shooting.

From behind us came the greatest surprise; a Polish cavalry group with extended sabers galloping between us. They shouted a great "hurrah!" and disappeared in to the trees in front.

In a short while some of the fifty riders who attacked on horseback started to come back. It was a tragic sight, some were running on foot,

some still upon their horses. Many of the soldiers were bleeding and fell on the way back to our line. We were still lying low, no shots had been fired.

We could see the SS Storm Troopers, running from tree to tree and shooting in our direction, coming closer and closer. Suddenly, in the clearing ahead, there were Germans everywhere. They were walking and firing short bursts from their Schmeisers. A minute passed. Tension was growing. I could see that their faces were covered with black paint, only the whites of their eyes were clearly visible.

"Ognia!" [Fire!] came the clear voice of our CO.

As our machine gun, along with all the other guns, opened fire, the Germans started to fall. Some of them tried to retreat but were cut down by the intense cross fire. As we were gaining control, our beautiful machine gun, the pride of our battalion had JAMMED! Swearing and quick servicing did not help.

"Withdraw," came the new order.

We were lucky. We had caused so many casualties among the enemy that they did not follow us.

"It is my turn to carry the ammunition box, so here is OUR bread" I said to Zbyszek. "Guard it with your life!"

We crawled backward the few feet down the hill. We did not have to worry. No bullets followed our retreat and we started to form a regular column and marched deeper into the forest. We had suffered no casualties and everything seemed to be in order. For hours we marched at a quick pace, listening to the distant sounds of the battles raging, never near enough to put us in danger.

Toward evening we stopped at a little village near the edge of the forest. We could no longer hear the sounds of the battle and everyone relaxed a bit. Some of the men managed to persuade a farmer's wife to cook some soup with a few vegetables. Finally we would have a decent meal.

In all the commotion and warfare, Zbyszek lost the big bread, and we had nothing to eat. The superstition of "the red bull" came true with many dead on both sides and the partisan division not getting together for a conference. It was an unforgettable time in the Polish mountains called Gory Swietokrzyskie.

Chapter 13

FOREST HIDEOUT

Methodically, the Germans were searching village after village for any signs of partisans in the area, so although we would have liked to remain there, we were ordered to pack up and move deeper into the forest.

During this time one of the men went to a water well. It was a roughly cemented four-feet-tall round ring of stones. He leaned his Mauser rifle against the stones and started to draw up a water bucket. To his horror, he saw his weapon slide down the cemented wall. The gun fired as it hit the ground. The man was stunned and had a strange sensation of warmth and itchiness on one of his legs. At first he did not realize that the shot had hit him in the back of his leg and being a Dum-Dum bullet, had ripped off lots of the muscle and flesh. Fortunately, his tendons and bones were left intact.

As the shot rang out, everyone grabbed their guns and jumped up. Some of us, realizing what had happened, ran to him. He was in pain, moaning and vomiting, and we laid him on the ground. We all looked in horror at the results of the unfortunate accident. It was very serious and we realized that a stretcher was needed. We were in the middle of wilderness. None of the backwoods farmers had anything like that. It had to be made from the materials available on the spot.

Our attention and sympathy was interrupted by a sentry who arrived, out of breath, having run from somewhere in the direction of the main road.

"Why did you shoot a gun?" he gasped. "A passing German column heard it and they are heading in our direction. We had better scramble!"

Quickly orders were given. A horse and wagon were requested. Two young spruce trees were chopped and attached to the wagon to drag and camouflage the tracks. Everybody was frantically packing. The injured man was put on the simple four wheel lorry with wooden wheels. We tried to make it as comfortable as possible with some straw. We moved out fast, again leaving soup still cooking in its big milk container, which the farmer was hiding so any evidence that a group of partisans had visited them was removed.

Our medical doctor had something for the pain but nothing to dress the injuries. The wounded man's sores were exposed and we hoped we could get him to a hospital. He lay in the wagon with his naked leg bent. We could see the tendons moving back and forth, no flesh remaining to cover them.

Our attention was drawn to the distant horizon as we neared the forest. The commanding officer stopped, looked through his big binoculars and after scanning the horizon for a few moments said quietly:

"The sons of a bitch sure are coming."

I was right beside him, and he said:

"Olek, do you want to have a look?"

"Yes, Sir" I replied quickly. I set the box of the MG 42 ammunition at my feet, and eagerly took the binoculars.

Sure enough, over the little hill and at the bend of the road they were coming, one lorry after another, a solid mass of German steel helmets and grey battle uniforms. They were not SS however, they looked more like the regular Wehrmacht troops. I even saw the well known Panzer Mark IV tank.

"Sir, they are bringing in the tanks," I reported with an excited voice. The CO quickly took the binoculars. I grabbed my ammo-box and ran after the others. We marched and marched, deeper and deeper into the forest, changing directions and pausing now and then to listen.

One good thing about a machine gun carrying crew was that we did not have to go on patrol or on reconnaisance in front of the column. Many of our patrol comrades had been killed when they unexpectedly met some Germans. I was positioned right in the middle of the column. The horse drawn wagon with the injured man was at the very back. The trees dragging from behind removed all our tracks. It was relatively easy to make impressions in the mostly sandy soil in the woods but it was also quite easy to erase them.

We were in a large forest divided every kilometer or so by wide paths going north-south and east-west. The CO ordered our unit into one of these large sections of forest. As the noise of shooting and other related sounds grew in intensity, we cut through the bush and into the centre of our hideout. The men at the end of the column made sure that there were no tracks left behind us. In a short while we heard armored vehicles on the path we had just left. They were making so much noise that it gave us time to find depressions in the ground and cover up with branches and hide.

"Everybody find a place and lie down," whispered the CO. "No noise of any kind or I will shoot the sonofabitch. No fires or smoking! The Germans can smell it in the forest and if they find us we are done."

We understood the seriousness of the situation and everyone did his best to be quiet. Our biggest problem was the horse. We grabbed some rags and sacks and made a big funnel and stuck it over his head. However, the horse was remarkably quiet and caused us no problems.

It was evening and everybody was exhausted. We slept in such a way that we could see and hear each other to be sure no night noises were made. The Germans disappeared and all was quiet.

I was lying in my little cavity, richly padded with thick, soft and green moss and dreaming.

One summer many years ago, we went to that rustic country village, Jezioro to spend a few weeks in rural surroundings. I would have been ten or eleven years old at that time. Dad had the use of an army truck to take us there. I remember that its back was covered with a green tarp, there were eight or nine of us, two families. We had lots of fun sitting in the back of the truck on side benches. Somebody hung a

straw picnic basket in the middle of the roof and the basket, full of
goodies, swung from side to side on the bumpy road.

As we travelled along the dusty roads, we enjoyed all the
sandwiches and cookies our mothers had prepared. Stories were told
and songs sung. As we approached the village we lifted part of the
tarp, the day was very warm. The dirt road had turned into pure sand
so it was no longer so dusty. The winding country road stretched
through some forests with beautiful, big trees on both sides. The forest
opened and the widening road followed the natural curves of the
terrain. We went down a small slope toward the village. It had only one
street made of pure, clean, yellow sand. The houses lined both sides of
the road, every one had a white picket fence and two gates. One gate
was for people and a larger one for wagons and cattle. Our driver blew
the horn and some children came running to open the big gate.

The unloading and greetings between ourselves, the farmer and his
wife and children took place. I saw a group of village kids half hiding
behind the side fences and watching, with great curiosity, all the
activity. They were shy but curious.

The house we were staying at was very low set. It had a traditional
straw roof and small but beautiful, picturesque windows with sill-
boxes

*full of blooming flowers. On the street side a little garden was planted
with its own picket fence and a tiny gate. The house doors were flung
open and we were ushered in. We had to step down to get through the
door into a large kitchen furnished with a long, handmade table and
two benches. The ceilings were low. The dirt floor was as hard as
concrete as a result of thousands of feet that had passed through the
door. All the walls and the stove were freshly whitewashed with a
mixture of lime and blue. The scent of smoke from the wood burning
stove added to its beauty. The farmer slept behind the kitchen stove
where he had a niche with a nice, straw filled mattress. It was a warm
and cosy place and also the closest to the entrance door, for ease in
bringing more wood or going out to do chores or defending the house
against intruders. Primitive wooden doors lead to the other rooms. The
gifts we had brought from the big city were received with happy
laughter. We had dinner at the big table in the kitchen.*

*At dusk, the children were taken to the hayloft in the barn. We
were to sleep and then were instructed about the danger of candles and
fires. Fortunately, we had a flash light. I remember, it was flat with a
flat battery and a thick, convex glass lens at one end. Occasionally the
batteries failed and it left us fearful in the dark. Our beds were made
up and in the quickly approaching dark our parents kissed us
goodnight and left us alone. The sweet smell of hay was heavenly. We*

told each other scary stories until late. Gradually, one by one, we fell asleep just as I now fell asleep in the partisan forest.

Next morning there was no line-up. The officers quietly counted people and exchanged information as we sat in a big circle. The only food supply we had was a one hundred litre milk can full of honey. The bread I had guarded so carefully had disappeared somewhere en route. There was no water available. Somewhere deep in my sack was the half piece of a smoked sausage. We had no choice but to begin plans to move out.

Our plans were foiled as we heard trucks arriving and the soldiers unloading. We heard them checking square after square of forest. Sometimes we could hear them going right into the trees, other times they just walked around firing an occasional shot into the bush. It was almost impossible for them to check every meter in the many kilometers of dense woods.

It was remarkable how sound carried in the big forest. Once in a while, we could hear clearly what the German soldiers were saying. Just like over water, there are many mysterious echoes between the trees. The search lasted most of the day and into the night. It sounded like the Germans were bivouacking on the paths all around us. We had some moments of suspense when we heard one of the Germans fumbling through the bush not far from us. It was getting dark and he approached close to us before he went back to his friends. I heard him say:

"Ludwig, wo bist du?"

He shouted a few times, obviously looking for somebody.

That was a close call. A battalion of about seventy men sat absolutely still and survived only because it was not yet their time. The next day the Germans returned, still searching. They never entered our square, but occasional shots whistled between the branches to remind us that it was not over.

By the third day, the little cavity we used as a latrine, was full of human excrements. It had began to look and smell like honey. On the fourth day the men were offering anything, even their gold rings, for a piece of bread or a glass of something to drink. Nobody had anything, we were all in the same boat. The smell of honey was everywhere. It was morning of our fifth day of concealment in the woods when a miracle happened. The forest fell silent. For the fourth time I escaped death.

We took no risks. One of the younger guys, dressed like a local peasant, without any papers or a weapon, was sent to explore. He was gone for many hours. He returned with some bottles of water and some bread. Everybody got a tiny little bite of bread but the water went to the injured man and to the horse.

Our reconnaissance man had good news: the Germans had left the area during the night deciding that we must have somehow slipped through their blockade. There were no more troops in the neighborhood and we could safely move out .

Tired and hungry we marched in a miserable column. The horse was still walking even though he had no water for many days. We all patted him for being so quiet and thus saving our lives. We dropped our injured man at a primitive medical centre run by Polish personnel.

We were ready and able to continue our struggle.

Chapter 14

A FINAL MISSION

Something was tickling my nose as I slowly opened my eyes.

The only sound was a lazy bumble-bee buzzing in the sweet smelling, fall, ripe wild grasses. It was hovering gently under my nose, just loud enough to wake me up. Raising my head and looking around I saw my young friends lying in the most uncomfortable positions, snoring softly in the morning sun. Some were holding their weapons. Some had their guns leaning against a bush or a tree trunk.

My feet were aching. The old rags I had wound around them were full of holes. There was no such luxury as a pair of socks. Sores on my heels and by my toes were bleeding and infected. I would have to do something about them.

In the distance, I heard the sound of a labouring engine.

"Psst - wake up, something is coming."

Heads started to rise instantly and few of the guys ran up the hill to take a look from the slope that faced the winding country road.

"No shooting without orders and make damned sure nobody sees you," ordered the CO.

As the vehicle came closer, tension grew. One of the partisans gave the square signal, used to identify the Germans. No shots were fired. They came down from the observation post announcing that it was a jeep with four Germans soldiers. One of the young men addressed our commanding officer.

"Why didn't you let us destroy them, Sir?"

The CO explained that the Germans had great numbers of troops in the area. We had to be very careful not to draw attention. One vehicle and four Germans missing could bring a massive search and attack.

"It is better to plan several attacks simultaneously so that the Germans do not know our precise location or our numbers," said the CO.

With that explanation we made a small fire and boiled some coffee. A few loaves of bread were divided and some pieces of smoked bacon distributed. We were lucky that day, we had something to eat.

The CO called Zbyszek and myself and another guy named Jan. After breakfast two comrades and I were sent on an undercover mission.

"You three go to the village in the valley, find the Mayor and ask him to secure food, enough to feed one hundred men. Have them collect and deposit the supply on the outskirts of the village. We will pick it up tonight after dark." He handed me the requisition form.

Zbyszek, Jan and I walked down the path. Both of them had Stenguns which they hid under their jackets. I had a rifle too big to hide. I carried it horizontally in my hand, as low as possible making sure that nobody could see it. We walked through the bushes and around the bends when we saw the first house a couple of hundred meters away. A big, black mutt of a dog, uncombed and ugly, spotted us and barked loudly.

Zbyszek and Jan continued, walking casually like two farm boys until they disappeared behind the house. The dog stopped barking. Nobody whistled a warning, everything seem to be safe. I followed them, holding my rifle as low as possible and not as ready for action as I normally would be.

I rounded the the corner of the building.

A clear strong voice, in perfect Polish said. . . "Drop your rifle! Raise your hands up!"

*

We were back at the execution site, here - deep in the Polish mountains.

My eyes were closed when I heard a long series of a machine gun fire and some shouting. More shots were fired but nothing seemed to happen to my body, no pain and no different feeling.

"Is this the way we die? No pain of any kind? It must happen so quickly, that we do not feel any thing. Maybe I am in heaven now?"

Cautiously, I opened my eyes. I had the strongest ever feeling that a new life of mine had just commenced. This belief has remained so strong in me since then that many years later I decided to begin this Book of my Lives with that absolutely miraculous rescue.

The three young Germans were lying on the ground. A group of partisans were searching their bodies and taking their weapons. I could not believe my eyes. They had saved us at the deadly last minute. The guys were laughing, talking, swearing and dancing. The CO had cleverly sent another group right after us.

Some of the village people came out of hiding. They carried the German bodies to a hole, stripped off their clothing that was burned in a dugout. The naked bodies were buried under a pile of cow manure so that no evidence of their existence would be visible and no odour discernable.

We helped the people gather some food at the edge of the forest, covering it with branches and leaves, ready for the night pick-up. Then, still shivering from the excitement, we went back to the forest.

* * *

We were deep in the Swietokrzyskie Mountains. Winter, and with it colder weather, was approaching. Usually the whole operation was dismantled as very few people could survive the forest in the winter. The hazard was doubled. If we did not freeze to death, tracks in the snow would give our locations away to the Germans. Many small battles were being fought with the Germans in this area. After our escape from the heaviest concentration of troops we were dodging through different forest zones, attacking here and there, escaping and hiding time after time.

One last operation was to be completed before we left the mountains. Our troop was to blow up a German transport train. The commanders went to work. Maps were obtained and the terrain studied so a suitable spot could be found. Patrols were sent in all directions to bring information and our little short wave battery radio was monitored day and night. London often gave instructions between news and music. Information that only the most experienced of us knew how to read. After much planning, a location for the ambush was chosen.

The morning of our raid dawned bright and clear. For just a fleeting moment our group of young patriots could almost imagine that the cruel war was a very bad nightmare. However, the terrifying truth of the situation reasserted itself as we marched to the chosen site. We had borrowed some trucks to follow us in case we were forced to retreat quickly.

Unfortunately, we did not have any mortar or grenade launchers so our heaviest weapons consisted of two machine guns. The "Filipinka" bombs with the heavy explosives were quite powerful weapons. Some of the men had Stenguns but most of us were equipped with regular military rifles. One of our soldiers sat in the yellowing bush to assemble the harness used to detonate the TNT. Two others were down the hill by the railroad tracks quickly digging a hole and burrying the dynamite and the detonators. They unrolled the long wire. The rest of us, formed a line with one machine gun on each end. Everyone was camouflaged in the best possible way.

"We had better place a few "Filipinkas" along the railroad and half way up this hill," said the CO. "You never know how things may turn out. The bombs will slow them down in case they decide to come after us."

A few of us grabbed a bunch of "Filipinkas" and walked down towards the railroad tracks. We placed the bombs randomly, removing the safety pins and covering them with leaves and grass. We finished quickly and we could hear, in the distance, the whistle of the big steam locomotive and the sound of the approaching train.

Back in position, well hidden we waited, with excitement and anticipation, for the arrival of the train. According to the intelligence reports, it was supposed to be a combined troop and supplies transport. Minutes passed and we almost thought that something had happened to the train. It had a winding track to negotiate, most of it up hill, so it took longer than expected. Finally it came into view: a big, shiny steam-engine pulling a long train of cars behind. We were appalled to see ahead of the engine an open box car full of German Wehrmacht soldiers with rifles. We had not anticipated this; our plans had to be changed quickly.

"Adam," whispered the CO "try to get the surprise off under the Germans in front but also try to make the locomotive jump the tracks! Everybody hide, they must not see us." What he meant was to detonate the mine right under the first car full of German troops.

The train came steadily around the big curve, getting closer and closer to our location and to the place where the mine was planted.

The explosion rocked the ground! In a split second I saw a great ball of fire, not from the boxcar in front, but from under the rear end of the steam engine. The impact sent the engine off the tracks. It was followed by several cars, some of them toppling over. Other cars, like in a slow motion movie, pushed by the momentum, rolled on top of them. This was heavy stuff. Fires started in some of the derailed cars.

Our guns were still quiet. Some of the Germans were shooting but they could not see anything to shoot at. We were well hidden by our camouflage so they were shooting in all directions.

The soldiers in the front boxcar, which did not turn over, were ordered out. Their purpose was to attack the enemy. As soon as they jumped down they began to run up on both sides of the hill, searching for us, the culprits. In the chaos, one of the fillipines exploded sending some soldiers up into the air. The rest quickly sought cover. Further along the tracks some soldiers tried to get an armoured vehicle down from one of the stranded box cars.

"Ognia!," rang the command of our leader and the whole line opened fire. The Germans retreated but not for long. Their first mortar exploded right below our lines. There were too many of them and they were much better equipped then we were.

"Stop firing and retreat," shouted the commander. The Germans were shooting at us with a sporadic but strong fire. The "Filipinkas" would slow them down should they started to follow us.

It was time for us to withdraw. We had done our job. Some of the enemy were dead, some of their equipment ruined and one of the rail lines out of commission.

We crawled backwards from our positions and began to run when we were behind the ridge. Everybody was breathing heavily by the time we reached our trucks. We quickly loaded, the drivers roared away getting out of sight of the Germans. We did not want the vehicles identified and reported to other troops or to the Luftwaffe.

The half hour speedy drive through some bushy countryside brought us back to where we had started. We unloaded and helped refill the trucks with the potatoes left on the side of the road.

"Boys, that was a job nicely done. Thank you all and let us pray to the Lord."

For a minute or two, everybody knelt with their helmets and hats off, and we followed the commander as he prayed,

"Our Father, Who Art in Heaven..."

The trucks drove away. We checked the ground and removed all signs of our passing. We marched back into the bush.

This event marked the end of my couple of months long participation in the "Ponury" battalion's harassment of the Germans. Winter was setting in, the evening was chilly. Some of us started two fires in order not to freeze one side of the body while sleeping in the cold air of the Polish mountains.

It had been a productive and exciting experience - however it was time for me to move on.

Chapter 15

MOTHER

A cold wind blew yellow leaves off the forest trees making a carpet design on the ground. The bonfire, although bright did not warm our backs. The partisans huddled and blew on their hands. Most of us had no gloves or winter clothing and we were wet, dirty and freezing. It was time to return to Warszawa. I hoped that by now the Gestapo would have forgotten about me and I could try to live there to the end of the war. I was released from my unit.

I did not tell the commander but I took a small weapon, just in case I needed it. I could not take a gun, but we had a few homemade grenades. They were apple size balls cast in lead with a wick that could be lit with a match or a burning cigarette. Sometimes they exploded right away and mostly never. I put one in my pants pocket and slid a few large onions on top of it for camouflage. The stand and the ammunition box I had been carrying for a couple of months stayed behind. Zbyszek remained as he wanted to stay with the boys a little longer while deciding what to do next.

It was the first of November 1943 and I have been with partisans for about two months. I said, "Goodbye to all of you, let's hope we meet again," as we hugged and kissed on both cheeks in the European men's manner. Another fellow and I started the long walk to the railroad station. After leaving the woods we whistled to keep up our courage.

We reached a village with a station. We were proud that without meeting the Germans we accomplished this. How naive of us it was not to know that the Germans had a "foolproof" way of identifying the "Boys from the Woods." They simply smelt them and if they smelled of smoke this was a 99% guarantee they had come from the forest. But, what you do not know cannot worry you.

After waiting with a bunch of other people, the overloaded train arrived. We pushed really hard to get on, and the journey home started. At one of the stations Gestapo and Schutzpolitzei agents ordered everybody off, car by car, and searched them.

I wanted to get rid of my grenade but could not think of how to dispose of it. If they found it lying on the floor they might shoot many innocent people. After more shouting and harsh commands before they came as far as our car, everyone again boarded. The train had to move to make room for a transport catching up behind it.

Near Warszawa there was more traffic on the roads. Someone told me that at the downtown Main Station, the Germans now searched and checked ID cards. I did not want to be checked, especially with my forged ID. I decided to get off at the big Okecie airport. Even with a few kilometers to walk I would still be able to get home before dark and the curfew hour.

Other people did the same thing. The station was not very big and there were only few Wehrmacht Military Police. They did not make an official search. Some people loaded with parcels were stopped and probably robbed of their supplies. I moved past them unchallenged. I was not carrying anything except my pocket full of onions.

"Halt!"

What was the matter? I had already passed them. My heart beat faster.

"Was hast du hier?" a big, Wehrmacht soldier pointed to my pocket with the muzzle of his rifle.

"Oh, I only have some onions," I answer trying to keep my voice steady.

"Zeig mir," [Show me] said the soldier.

It felt like an eternity. I pulled out one onion and he came closer stretching out his hand. I handed him the onion and he waved for more. He

was putting the first one in his side bag while his comrades, a few meters away were stealing other people's parcels. I slowly handed him another onion.

"How many onions do you have?" asked my searcher. He must have felt sorry for me because seeing in my pant pocket only two more bulges of the "onions", he waved me on my way. I do not know if I should have cried or jumped with happiness.

As soon as I had crossed a farmer's field and reached some bushes I got rid of my "metal onion." I felt much better not carrying the ridiculous gadget which often did not work. I did not have any contact with my underground friends so there was no way of handing it to them. It was getting dark and the cold wind was howling. I hurried so I would not be out after the forbidden hour. Not many people were on the streets. Reaching my house I prayed that my mother would be home.

She was! The electricity was cut early in the evening. She cried, hugging and kissing me in the dark. Immediately, I had a warm bath, the first in two months. Then we sat and ate in the semidarkness and she asked lots of questions. She told me that Dad had been arrested a week after I left. They came for him one early morning. That was the first news I had about him and it made me very sad. If only he had listened.

"How was the forest life?" Mother asked .

"Well, we had a few battles and we sang a lot around the campfire," I answered, trying not to worry her too much.

"You had better sleep with me tonight. You never know when the Germans might come," she said. Her bed was ready, the others were not made up. She must have had a premonition because shortly after midnight there was loud banging on the downstairs door.

"Alex, get up! Here are your clothes! Come quickly!" She lead me to Dad's office and opened the window. We were on the second floor and it was pitch dark outside.

"Let's hope they don't have a dog with them," she said as she helped me escape through the narrow window parapet.

"Jump, don't wait! They are on the way up. My prayers are with you."

She gave me a quick push and closed the window tightly.

I leapt over four meters and landed on a small roof in the backyard. Fortunately, I did not break a leg, but only skinned my hands and legs.

As quietly as I could I went behind a chimney in hope it would hide me should they start looking in my direction. Peering carefully around it,

I saw the beam of a flashlight checking all the covered windows. There were some loud voices, but no dog barking. "How lucky can you be?", I thought to myself. I had once again escaped.

After what seemed to be forever, I could hear boot footsteps in the stairway, the opening and slamming of the front gate and the starting of motors. In a couple minutes they were gone.

I squatted soundlessly on the little roof. The family of Volksdeutches were living in the apartment under this roof. I wondered if it was they who reported me that evening. I was thankful that very few people had telephones in those days. Imagine the harm they could cause me, because I am sure they must have heard my jump and my walking on their roof.

"Psst, Alex, come up," Mother was in the same window I had jumped from. The back door was not locked. Still holding my clothes and wearing my pyjamas I got up.

"Somebody must have seen you because they have not been here for months," said Mom.

"I am so glad we fooled them this time, but now, it is better that you pack and go somewhere far away from here. It isn't safe for you here any longer."

Quietly we started to go through my few belongings making a little bundle. Farewells were short and tearful knowing that it might be a long while before we met again. We discussed some possible places I could go and we chose the home of friends we have not seen for years.

I did not see my Mother again until she visited my new family in Norway around 1956, thirteen years later. She was so proud of our new baby, her little grandson Robert, calling him:"Taki duzy, taki duzy," [so big, so big]. We were right on that dark, frightful night years back in Warszawa.

Chapter 16

OSTROWIEC SWIETOKRZYSKI

The streets were empty. I had avoided the German patrols. I walked to a friend's house a few streets away and rang the bell.

"Who is there?" a voice cried from behind the heavy door.

"This is Alex Jadach from Narbutta Street. Could I please come in? It is very important that I come in right away."

"What...what happened? Why do you visit people at this hour? This is still the curfew hour, you know."

"We had some problems with the Germans; they came to arrest me and I had to run away. Let me in and I can tell you all about it."

"No, we don't want you, go away! It is dangerous to help people like you these days. Go away and don't bother us!"

"Please, I need help."

"No, go away, don't involve us."

Stranded in Warszawa, the people I trusted would not help. I walked to a little clump of bushes and sat on the ground. What should I do now? Where should I go? I had some money but where and how could I hide myself?

"Ostrowiec Swietokrzyski," I almost shouted the words out loud. Kosicki, a school friend of mine, Stanislaw Kosicki, lived at his parents' home there and would do anything to help me. I was sure of that.

I remained hidden in the bush until the curfew hours ended. I went to the Central Railroad Station, paid a bribe and got a ticket to Ostrowiec.

Sitting on the train I was dreaming about my country being free again. I dreamed about the old days when family parties, especially at Christmas, brought happy memories. Once, when I was six or seven years old, I got a soldier's drum with shoulder crossing white belts. I stood guard walking back and forth in front of the entrance, drumming marching rhythms and waiting for "Swiety Mikolaj" [Santa Claus]. Laughter came from the dining room where the guests and the family had gathered for the celebration. They shouted my name and said that Santa must have changed his mind and came in through the

balcony. All the presents were there! I could not figure it out. I was
disappointed not to have met "Swiety Mikolaj" that year.

These warm memories helped to make the war easier. The journey to
Ostrowiec did not take long.

I was intrigued by what I found. My friend's dad had been arrested by
the Germans and put in a concentration camp. This seemed the fate of all
active Polish officers. Stanislaw, my friend, had a younger sister Mila
who was a terribly spoiled child. His mother was a slim, beautiful,
sophisticated woman. I was received with open arms.

She was heavily involved in the resistance movement and knew
everybody in town. She got me a job immediately as a messenger in the
German controlled Tax Department. The job was significant because
people who worked in the Taxation Department were not often sent to
forced labour. I was trained to deliver tax demands to the population of
the area. I was given a bicycle to make deliveries. I did not realize what I
was getting into. Bicycling to the other end of town to deliver a demand-
letter for overdue taxes sounded simple. Many of the people tried to avoid
paying their taxes while attempting to remain in favor with the
department.

I was young and naive. I was invited in, offered the best of food and
schnapps and treated like a king. The ladies smiled and the men made rash
promises. They hoped I would help them avoid or postpone payment or
put in a good word with the boss.

The delivery job was a cover. What I was really doing was transporting
illegal Press. There were several undercover printing presses in the
district. Almost every day, I carried a large bag full of weekly or monthly
bulletins from the Underground. They were spread among the population
and the different organizations.

One day, I went to see a man who lived in a run-down farmhouse on
the outskirts of the town. His dog barked ferociously inside the house and
I didn't know what to do. His bill for several hundred zloty was overdue
and I was ordered to collect that day or else.

"Who is there?" said an inquiring voice when I knocked on the heavy
door.

"This is Marian, a messenger from the tax department."

"What do you want?" he yelled rudely.

"I am here to talk to you about the seven hundred zloty you owe in back taxes, Mr. Godzielski, may I come in?" The door was rapidly opened and the man, shabbily dressed and unshaven was all in smiles.

"Please come in, what we have we shall share with you. Please, please, come in. Go away you stupid dog." His kick at the dog did not reach the animal, "go and lie down and don't bother nice people."

I went into a sparsely furnished kitchen. Coffee was on the stove and something else was cooking on the other burner. The warmth was welcoming after the cold bike ride. Mr. Godzielski brushed a messy chair clean and insisted that I sit down. His daughter came in and curtsied. Mr. Godzielski sent her for a bottle of moonshine from the cellar.

"I do not drink" I said.

"Oh no, you can not say that, you must take a shot with me, I insist."

"Well, I do not drink and especially when I am on duty."

"Nonsense, we cannot discuss business before we have a little drink and something to eat. "Mary," he turned to his daughter again, "run back to the basement and bring a piece of smoked bacon and a loaf of that good bread mother baked last week." He waved her away with his hands, rushing her on her way to accomplish these tasks.

"Mr. Marian, how nice of you to come and see me," he continued. With a big smile he filled two glasses to the brim with the vodka.

"Na zdrowie!" [To your good health], he tipped his head backward and emptyied the glass in one shot.

"For Christ sake, why don't you drink with me?" he added. He broke a large piece of the homemade bread and cut a chunk of bacon with his pocket knife.

"Come on, I cannot do business without a drink. You are old enough to have a drink with me, eh?"

He sat down and fumbled in a drawer for some documents.

"Here," he said "it says right here that I owe seven hundred zloty and eleven groszy. This is a BIG chunk of money with my little shoe business. You know the bosses in the tax department, you can talk to Mr. Kunicki and convince him that old Godzielski don't get rich on making shoes. Ask him for me, eh, to reduce this chunk of money?"

"Now you must take a shot of this excellent brew. I made it myself and it is the best in the valley." He grabbed my glass and forcefully held it in front of my mouth.

Knowing Polish customs, I had no choice. I took a little sip and almost choked. Those guys were not fooling around. This was potent stuff probably made from fermented potatoes. Strong and not diluted, just pure alcohol.

"Here, you take this, one hundred zloty from me to Mr. Kunicki. You give it to him, tell him to keep it and not to send more demands for a while, OK?"

I had barely regained my breath.

"You cannot do this. It is bribery and the department will not approve of it."

It was like talking to a wall.

"You know Mr. Kunicki, you work there, you talk to him. He is nice, ya, nice like you. You give him this 100 zloty, tell him to send it back if he don't want it."

Another day, I was carrying a large suitcase of illegal bulletins out of the government building. It broke open and hundreds of pieces of underground literature fell to the sidewalk. A German SS who worked in one of the offices, and recognized me as a messenger, was just behind me. I stiffened sure that this was the final hour of Alex Jadach, alias Marian Chmielowicz.

Good fortune was still on my side. The soldier did not know Polish at all. He bent down and helped me put all the papers back into my suitcase.

HE THOUGHT THEY WERE GERMAN GOVERNMENT DOCUMENTS!

We picked up every one of them and he said in German: "Ask them to give you a better bag for carrying government forms. If it had been wet you would have lost most of them. Saying "Heil Hitler," he walked away.

It was a hectic life and patriotic things were done nearly every day. I was young and I needed to do something more. I decided that the best solution for me was to go back to Warszawa. Somehow, I would try to get in touch with my old cell and look for more exciting assignments. I really had nowhere to go.

Back in Warszawa, in the spring of 1944 , I stood at the entrance of the Central Railroad Station and looked out at the big street with all the people and all the overwhelming traffic.

A man, with two medium sized suitcases, came past me out of the station. He crossed the wide street to the narrow tramway island, stopped in the middle and set his luggage. He reached in his jacket pocket, got out some tobacco and cigarette paper and started to roll himself a smoke while waiting for the tram to arrive. He took out his matches and turned slightly to one side, to shield from the wind. He tried to light his cigarette. At the same moment I saw a young, husky boy, come behind him. The boy grabbed one suitcase from behind his back and ran away.

It took a while for the man to light his cigarette. Satisfied, he took several large puffs, put away the matches and rubbed his hands with pleasure in the cool wind. The tram arrived and the man bent down to lift his two suitcases. His reaction was a comedy pantomime as he tried to understand what had happened to one of his luggage. There was nobody else on the island. With one suitcase in his hand he ran back and forth, looking here and there. The boy was long gone.

Although I felt very sorry for him, he looked comical. I was too far away to shout or do anything to create commotion or to attract attention. I laughed to myself and in a better mood I walked down the street.

Deep in my thoughts, I did not realize what was happening. LAPANKA! "Lapanka" was a term used to mean "the catch." What the Germans did, on a regular basis, was cordon off a couple of blocks. They searched everybody within the area. If your papers did not indicate you were important to the Third Reich, or that you held a job which was vital, you were sent to forced labour somewhere far away from your home.

Several of us were loaded into a "buda" and driven to a nearby encampment.

When we arrived at the barbed wired barracks we were ordered to undress and take a shower while our clothes were disinfected. Stark naked, we were taken to a big gym and lined up in front of a doctor wearing a white frock.

The doctor was using a large pair of wooden pincers to lift and examine our penises to make sure we had not been circumcised. The Germans did this as a way of identifying people of Jewish origin.

Back in our compartment, we were dozing off, while waiting. To forget what I just went through, I was day-dreaming an unrelated memory about my geography teacher back in the good old days. Sometimes some of the students in my public school were invited to visit this teacher whom we thought fascinating. He had curly gray hair and a bushy mustache. His home was full of collections of all kinds, stones and frogs in jars, maps from the four corners of the world and medical charts. He would take a huge magnifying glass and with the help of the light from an electric bulb, would look deeply into our eyes. He had large color charts on the wall explaining the human pupil. By the different "spots" in our eyes, their color and location, he was able

to tell us about our health and our habits. It was always an honour to
be invited to his place.

Early next morning we were loaded on trucks again and transported to
the city of Szczecin [Stettin] on the west Baltic coast, where we began
work for the Organization Todt (OT), as forced labourers for the
Germans.

The routine of the camp was soon established. Reveille at 5 a.m., eat
at 6 a.m. and work by 7 a.m. We were marched to different spots in the
city, to bombed buildings or other ruins, to clear the debris and sort out
salvageable items. At noon the standard bunker soup arrived. We had a
half-hour break to swallow the boiled water with a slight vegetable taste.
One was lucky if one ever found vegetables in it. A piece of black bread
went with it.

After the short rest it was back to work for long, hard afternoon until 6
o'clock when we marched back to the camp. In the evening we were quite
exhausted and went to bed early in our uncomfortable bunk beds. The
days went by.

Chapter 17

ESCAPE TO BERLIN. BERLIN YOU SAID?

Life became very monotonous after several weeks in the labour camp. My new friends and I started to discuss plans to escape. We wanted to join the war effort. That meant getting back to occupied Poland, or to the front in Italy (where Polish units were fighting), or a neutral country like Sweden or Spain. Once there, we could contact the allied forces who were winning in Africa and Italy, and recently in Normandy. The Warsaw Uprising which started on August 1, 1944 made us even more determined to get out of the camp. We were relatively safe, if you can call it safe being bombarded by the Americans during the day and the British during the night.

Our discussions were conducted whenever and wherever the opportunity arose. A group of us, former Boy-Scouts and highschool students tried to get on the same work team, so we could talk, and plan. We had to be on the lookout for informers. The place was full of them. Some of the Ukrainian or Slovakian workers, would do anything to gain favour with the Germans. There were also Polish spies. Many of them looked for an opportunity to get ahead

Most of our group understood German, a couple of us spoke it fluently. Once in a while, we got hold of a newspaper. Although full of propaganda, we could learn a few things.

We heard about a driving school outside Berlin. It trained truck drivers and somebody got the crazy idea of going to apply. Then, when driving trucks by the front line, wherever it was, we could try to escape to our side. That dream of escape became a real obsession and lasted, with several attempts to realize it, throughout the rest of the war.

Our escape plans were not complicated. We were sent to jobs without guards because we were on German territory. It was assumed no one would try to escape. Seven of us went to the railroad station and took the first train to Berlin. We just took off knowing that nobody would miss us before evening, or even, if we were lucky, not until early next morning.

There were no conductors and no one taking tickets. We slipped through with the rest of the crowd and boarded an over-crowded train.

The trains were full of German soldiers and a few civilians. We were wearing the Organization Todt striped pants and green caps with the Todt lettering, but without any German eagle insignia or, God forbid, swastikas. We hated that symbol. Except the working force sign, "O.T.", we had nothing else on our garments. There was a canteen car on the train where one could buy cheap beer, a salad or some soup. All these things were war products. The soup was thin, the salad full of weeds, roadside weeds! The Germans had brigades of older people who walked along the roads to gather dandelions and other edible greenery. These greens were used in the military kitchens in the preparation of food for thousands of travellers.

The beer was sour. As I was not used to different food I got quite ill. There were several others that were as sick as I was. Who knows what was put in the food to make it go further.

Early that afternoon, I was sitting on the floor in a corner of the hallway and dozing off, when a couple of strong, vibrating explosions shook the air. Immediately the brakes were applied, the train stopped and everything flew forward. Shouts and commands were given. People started to jump off the cars, rolled to the low ground and looked around. I jumped too and discovered that the train was on a tall mound.

At first I had no idea what had happened. Then I saw, right behind the train, many craters along the tracks and lots of smoke. Some soldiers were bleeding. I looked closely and could see many shrapnel holes in the sides of the rear cars.

Looking up, where people were pointing, I could also distinguish a group of small dots slowly fading away, high up in the sky, and leaving behind tiny, white lines of vapour. The boys who knew German explained to me that an American armada of high flying B-17's was apparently on its way to bomb something deeper in Germany. Flying over a moving train, some of the pilots could not resist dropping a few "pills." This time, I was glad the German train had not been directly hit.

After the injured were attended to, the train moved on. I sat on the floor, listening to the monotone and rhytmic noise of the wheels and started to day dream again.

The "Zug" was pressing on. It had taken most of the day and by late afternoon somebody pointed to a small station somewhere outside Berlin. We had an address to go by, so we left the train. I had only a rolled blanket over my shoulder and a little side bag which held all my earthly possessions. They were a couple of sheets of paper, since I always liked to write down some of my thoughts, my Ausweis ID Card, a beautiful Mont Blanc fountain pen given to me by my "Tatus" when I started high school in 1939, and a whole kilogram of finely cut Virginia type tobacco. These were my priced possessions. At that time, tobacco was one of the best trading items, even better then money.

My friends and I briskly walked through what looked like parklands with lovely big trees, ponds and small fields. Military convoys and a motorcycle, with a side car, driven by a helmeted SS with a submachine gun over his shoulder passed us. We later found out that we were in the vicinity of Hitler's underground bunker. These were the headquarters' messengers going back and forth. We were lucky that nobody had stopped us. We did not have any travelling papers or other documents giving us a reason to be in that particular location. German officers, even with their papers intact but without travel orders, were known to be shot on the spot.

We arrived at a barricade gate with guards and, after explaining our business, were led into a large compound consisting of many barracks. A uniformed soldier pointed to the barrack where we were supposed to stay. There were hundreds of people of many nationalities around us, all civilians, many females. The stories flew freely as the afternoon started to turn into evening.

"Don't you guys want to go to that barracks, there? The Gestapo have a bunch of Russian women and they are all taking a shower before their interrogation."

The boys got all excited and started to walk towards our barracks.

My heart stopped at the words "Gestapo" and "interrogation".

I asked the guy, "Do you have Gestapo here? I thought it was a school for truck drivers." We were walking back towards a barrack.

"Don't you know," he said "this camp is run by the Gestapo and they investigate all the people brought in here."

Running back to the others, I said to my friend Jan:

"You and Antoni must help me. I cannot stay here for the Gestapo interrogation, I wouldn't last a minute with my fake papers. Those guys are experts in these things. You two have to help me to get out of here!"

In the beginning they did not want to help. They had not seen women for a long time.

"For Christ sake, aren't you going to help me?" I shouted. "Time is running out. If I don't get out of here now I will never get out!"

They unwillingly abandoned their pleasant plan of watching naked females through the dirty windows and not too happily came with me. We walked to our barrack and went behind it, toward the fence. Until then I had not paid much attention to how the camp was constructed, but now I saw that we were faced with the type of fence seen in old cowboy movies, a fort palisade made of debark trunks of young trees, about 2 to 3 meters tall with the tops sharpened to a point.

How the hell was I going to get over that? I quickly weighed my chances. If I stayed I would probably never get out, they might have the list of wanted people and even a picture of me. I had to go, there was no other alternative.

Fear gives people strength. With the help of my two companions, in the growing darkness and trying to make a minimum of noise, I got over.

"Mighty God," I whispered back, but it was too late. I had already landed on the ground and faced ANOTHER palisade about 1 meter ahead. The path between showed footsteps and dog droppings in which I had landed.

"God help me," I thought to myself. I could not stay there, sooner or later a guard would come along with a big German Shepherd and that would be the end of me. This was even worse than being in the Stalag itself. They would have good reason to suspect someone caught between the fences.

I do not know how I got over that barricade. After struggling for a good while, I fell heavily in the deep grass on the other side of the fence. I did not lose any fingers or nails, but I had a couple of scrub sores and very painful arms and legs. I laid there panting quietly and wondered what would happen next. "I better get out of here," I said to myself.

Chapter 18

NEW EXPERIENCES

In the distance I could see the outline of some trees. It also seemed to me that I could hear the sound of a train. I started to walk. With every step I thanked God for giving me another chance in this world full of death and brutality.

The field was long and uneven, some of it was ploughed but mostly it was covered with clumps of wild grass. Nearing the trees I could see in the semidarkness, train tracks and a platform. I was approaching a train station in the suburbs of Berlin! I was sure it must be the subway on the above ground run in the outskirts of the city.

Then I noticed a man standing on the platform watching me intently. He was clad in a typical European raincoat, with large epaulets on his shoulders and he was wearing a hat. The hat was dark with a turned down brim. His collar was up. I sensed the Gestapo.

"Oh, God, not again," I thought to myself.

I crossed the track and jumped on the platform. Slowly the man approached me with both hands deep in his pockets. Nobody else was around. He addressed me in German:

"Did you just walk across that field?" he said pointing to the field just came from.

"Ja, mein Herr," I answered quickly wondering what kind of gun he had in his pocket. I was defenseless and my German was very poor.

"Don't you know that this field is mined?" asked the man. "There are big signs everywhere."

I froze again. The thought of my body being torn to pieces by a mine shattered me. I did not know if I should be happy and relaxed or scared. Thousands of thoughts raced trough my mind.

The stranger saw my hesitation and asked in a softer tone:

"What language do you speak?"

"Polish," I said looking straight at him. I had no choice, I thought, it will work or it won't. "Where are you heading?" asked the man in a broken Polish. I was not a bit surprised. In Europe, people often spoke several languages. It opens your horizons.

"I am trying to get to my OT camp in Stettin. I am in a work force and we are about to be shipped to Finland," I told him without blinking an eye.

He didn't ask me what I was doing in Berlin. His name was Otto and he suggested that since there were no trains to Stettin that evening, I was welcome to spend the night at his apartment at Alexander Platz in Berlin. The well known Alexander Square in Berlin which even I heard about. I still did not totally comprehend that I was in another country, with another culture and language. But I remembered my geography books.

His generous offer made me a little suspicious. I was exhausted and could not think of any other alternative. I only hoped that he was as friendly a man as he appeared to be. I accepted his invitation and he paid my ticket on the U-Bahn [underground train] back to Berlin. The modern, half empty train with subdued lights sped away on his track towards the center of the city. While we travelled he told me about his life.

"I am a member of the Gestapo, don't be afraid, I am not going to arrest you. The situation is starting to get tough here. The constant air raids, the British by night and the American by day have left the city in ruins. The huge apartment building where I live was hit two weeks ago leaving us without electricity or heat."

The train stopped briefly at each station. Few passengers got on or off. In the dim lights I could see few details. My companion continued in broken Polish:

"There are thousands of soldiers coming home for leave or trekking through for new assignments and there are scores of deserters and people lost like yourself. My job is to catch these individuals and bring them to the Police Station. There are also illegal weapon sales. Guns can be bought for next to nothing. I get paid a commission for arrests and weapon repossession." He did not explain why he was not in the army. I wondered why.

"The next stop is Alexander Platz and I will take you to my place. I have a Gestapo partner who lives with me, but tonight he is away." The train came to a noisy stop. The big sign in the surprisingly well lit underground station read: ALEXANDER PLATZ.

We came to a large town square, after a short walk. On one side of the square, in the semi darkness, I could see an enormous apartment block, five to seven stories tall. When we came closer, I saw that one side cascaded like a great mountain slide. The bomb must have been very powerful because several apartments had been levelled, gaping with open rooms, hanging pieces of furniture and pipes. It was something to see. We walked to the other end of the building and climbed the dark staircase.

"Do you like boys better than girls?" a voice asked. I could not really see him in the darkness but I heard the clicking boots ahead where the voice spoke to me. I followed as closely as possible. It was dark and I did not know where we were going. His question weighed heavily on my mind.

"Why do you ask that?" I stammered "what is your reason for asking such a stupid question?"

We stopped and I could hear him fumbling with the keys to the door. It was dark inside. He grabbed my shoulder and pulled me in gently.

"Wait a moment until I get some light." I stood there thinking about the massive destruction in the other parts of the building. I had seen bomb damage before but nothing like this. The American bombs must have been very powerful.

A dim light came from a doorway. "Come into the kitchen," said Otto. "We have to find something to eat." He prepared some food by the faint candle light and an oil-lamp.

"Do you have any brothers or sisters?" he asked quietly.

"No, I had a brother who died at the beginning of this bloody war. He was a pilot in the Polish Air Force."

He showed me the apartment. It was a comfortable flat with two or three bedrooms, an elegant dining room, a balcony and the small kitchen.

"This is my bedroom, would you like to sleep with me? You see, I like boys and you're such a nice looking guy that I thought I might keep you here for a while."

"No...no," I heard myself shouting. "That's something that does not appeal to me. I couldn't do anything like that." Without further persuasion he allowed me to sleep in the next bedroom. The room was free, his friend was away and would not be back until the following day.

"Tomorrow, I will help you get to the Stettin train," he continued. "By the way, if the air raid alarm goes off I shall not be going to the basement. I'll stay here and take my chances because I do not like the idea of being buried alive."

I had a quick wash in the bathroom with cold, running water. I placed my little side bag on the night table and went to bed. It was a comfort, a real bed where I could stretch out and it felt great.

I was disturbed with the days events. I had to dream again to forget. I began to recall how at another time, as if in another life, during one of our summer vacations, we, the kids, were sleeping in the hay loft and a rooster's crow woke us up. Roman was sleeping peacefully a few feet away. I remembered it was daylight so I got up and in my nightshirt and bare feet, climbed down from the hayloft and looked out through the open barn door. What a different view met my eyes. Not what I was used to in the big city. There was a horse grazing not far from me blowing through his nostrils every little while and a bunch of domestic ducks running around trying catching some small jumping frogs. The grass was covered with morning dew and the droplets of water shone like little diamonds. A big red rooster sat on a fence, regularly producing his wake-up sounds. Some pigs were snorting around on the ground behind him. There was so much to see. But I was getting chilly, so despite my interest, I trotted back up to the hayloft and buried myself in my bedclothes.

I think I fell asleep again because the next thing I was aware of was Roman, fully clad, standing beside me and asking:

"Would you like something to eat Alex?"

I quickly jumped up. In the yard the sun was already high in the sky. From the house the good smell of fried eggs and sausages hit my nostrils and I ran as quickly as I could to the kitchen.

I dream again... The farmer had gone to work in the field but after breakfast the farmer's wife took us around on a tour of the property. She showed us all the animals and the poultry and the corner of the house where the family made cheese from the milk produced by their cows.

At dinner time, we all sat around the large kitchen table. In the middle of the table stood an enormous, hand carved, wooden bowl with a huge heap of peeled, freshly cooked potatoes. Over the potatoes, the farmers wife slowly poured fried pork bacon cut into cubes. It smelled heavenly. We each had a wooden bowl filled with freshly made buttermilk and a wooden spoon to eat with. Everyone took a spoonful of the potato mixture from the bowl in the center of the table and then, from our own plate, a spoon of sour milk.

Then I drifted off. . .

When I woke up, Otto was standing at the foot of the bed. The blinds had been removed from the glassless windows and a cold breeze blew in the room.

"Sorry to wake you up, but I have some bad news. Someone robbed you last night. Your sack was on the floor, empty." Terrible, I thought, but I was putting on my pants and jacket as quickly as I could.

"What did you have in your bag?" he asked.

"One kilogram Virginia tobacco and my precious Mont Blanc fountain pen given to me by my father." He expressed his regret but he could not report the incident. He did not want the Gestapo to know that he was helping me.

"We must hurry if you are to make your train." We hurried down the stairs and rushed to the station. It had been heavily bombed. There were hundreds of people, mostly soldiers in uniforms and women saying goodbye to their loved ones. I boarded the train to Szczecin. Otto waved and smiled. I was thankful that my escape from the Gestapo compound cost me only a fountain pen and some tobacco. Things that could be replaced.

Late in the afternoon the train arrived in Szczecin and I became more frightened as I walked to the camp. I could think of no other alternative but returning to the camp. If I were picked up again, having no travelling papers, I would be in big trouble. The guard recognized me and pointed his gun at me. I had been missing for twenty four hours.

"Don't shoot, don't shoot, I am back," I pleaded in my broken German. He searched me, summoned another guard to take over, he marched me straight to the commandant's office.

"Where have you been? Where are the others? What have you been doing?" I had tried to prepare myself for this moment but in reality did not know what to say. Perhaps the best thing would be to stay as close to the truth as possible, I thought and started:

"It was their fault! I did not want to go but they said we would be trained as truck drivers. I really didn't want to go....", I whined, I hoped, convincingly.

"You stupid Polnische Dummkopf, we had to alert the Gestapo, we had all kinds of problems, du bist...." slap....slap.....slap.... across my face, my nose started to bleed. "You idiot, you don't just take off somewhere else without asking permission! The last thing we need is the Gestapo involved in our affairs!"

He made a phone call and a minute later two men appeared. They both wore the brown OT uniforms and had swastikas on their sleeves. He barked some quick commands and the two grabbed me roughly and led me to another barracks. There was a big room, empty except for a couple of chairs and a massive oak table, they started to beat me.

The same questions were asked over and over again. They continued to "Where did you go?"

It seemed like they would not believe my story. After another few minutes I was crying. The blood was pouring from my nose, mouth and split ear. Having repeated the same answers time after time, they suddenly stopped.

There was a bathroom attached to the room. One of them went in and brought back a wet towel and threw it to me.

"Here, clean yourself and return to your barracks. Tomorrow morning you better be punctual at the line-up or you're in a BIG trouble!" I leaned on the table, one hand rested on it to support my weight. I wiped the blood and tears from my face with the other hand.

Bent over, my back sore from the beating, I went to my barracks and found my old bunk. I laid down and thought about all that had happened in the last 24 hours. I did not sleep well, every bone in my body ached.

Early next morning, before the others were up, I went to shower. I was lucky, they still had hot water a couple of times a week.

I went out to the open stadium where our barracks were built. Despite my soreness I started to run around, the towel flying around my neck. The OT officer from the previous night came out: He hollered:

"Go and get dressed! You will have plenty of exercise today and every day from now on." He kicked me forcefully in my already painful back.

The workers were lined up and the commandant came out. In addition to the day orders, he recounted my story emphasizing how stupid I had been. He yelled that next time anybody tried something like that they would be shot on sight. He added that from now on, we would be assigned a personal guard, an older Wehrmacht soldier with a rifle. The guy was already there. He stepped forward and placed himself close to me. From that day he stayed with us wherever I went.

Later, a number of us were transported to Gdansk harbour to board a ship to Finland. The soldier was still my private "bodyguard." It became a joke among us, that I belonged to nobility and he had been assigned us as my private butler.

Chapter 19

THE SUGAR FACTORY

British and American bombers, flying at very high altitudes, were now wave-bombing the whole area. Concentrating on Szczecin, a harbour city, the Allies did their best to disrupt the Third Reich's transport system. The air was acrid with smoke from the burning factories and homes.

Every morning after the head count and a quick scanty breakfast we marched to the factories where the flames had subsided to the point that we were able to rescue some of materials and machinery.

One such assignment was a bombed sugar factory.

Three of the factory walls were barely standing, and there was no roof. The far corner of the enormous building was still smoldering. The machinery was burned and twisted. The tall brick walls had large, high metal window frames but no glass. The walls protected us from the brisk, marine wind. We did not have any warm clothes, but we were quite comfortable.

Our task was to save as many of the sugar sacks as possible. We sat on a mountain of jute sugar sacks, all water soaked, some burned, and surveyed the scene. There were some old lorries parked on the debris-strewn street. We systematically moved the least damaged of the water soaked bags. We slowly dragged or carried them to the street. My watchman left suddenly when an air raid alarm sounded. We just remained seated on the bags and hoped that the Yankees would see the burned out building and use their bombs on another target.

The day was clear but we could not see the bombers, only the air streams behind them. They were flying very high, and there were dozens coming our way. The explosions, following the bombers, were coming closer. The ground anti-aircraft fire was rapid but the canons could not reach the height of the approaching armada of bombers.

The German Luftwaffe's Messerschmidt planes were making big circles in an attempt to gain altitude before attacking. A small plane was hit by the gunners of an American Flying Fortress bomber. The plane started to burn and spin in a graceful circle downwards. Moments later we watched the pilot eject and his parachute open.

A whole forest of bombs was released from the heavy Boeings. They gurgled in the distance, filling the air with the sound of death. Fortunately they were quite a distance away and the formation took a slightly different direction and was no longer a threat to us.

I have always been a dreamer. Dreams are vital for survival especially under stress. Dreams are calming you and allow you to escape brutal reality. Dreams prepare you for upcoming events allowing you to rehearse the outcome. Out of nowhere, I began to dream about a centuries old type of flying: kites.

I remembered when my "Tatus" came from Warszawa to visit us at Jezioro. I would ask him if we could build a kite. This was one of my favorite pastimes. I was impressed that he could make kites from old newspapers, sticks and glue the string he brought from the city. We would stand in the middle of a field and fly the kites. On a windy day the kites would fly beautifully. As we gained experience, the kites became bigger and stronger. We coloured them and gave them faces and names. We became one with our kite.

Some days half of the village would come and participate.

But reality was here and now - no more pretending with kites. The kite crashed in my mind....

"If the Yankees get us here, it will be a sweet death," joked one of my companions.

We all laughed.

There was no escort protection for the American planes. All of them did their jobs and started to move away in a new direction. We had an incredible view of the air fight. The small Messerschmidt planes finally started to attack the retreating bombers. Some of the bombers were hit and some of the attackers also. More burning planes crashed into the ground.

We were so preoccupied watching the battle we did not notice a smaller wave of bombers approaching from the other side. All of a sudden tremendous vibrations shook the ground as the bombs exploded, and fires raged.

The noise was unbearable.

I was near one of the walls in danger of toppling over, I found a small hole where a few of the sugar bags had been removed and I lay down with my face stuck between two sacks. When the attack ended and the sound of the planes diminished, I stood up again. More of the city was burning, fire truck sirens were wailing. Glancing around, I saw a human arm sticking out from between the sugar bags. Minutes ago I was lying on top of him! Where I had taken shelter there was a dead body. I called my friends and we started to remove the bags. The odour was nauseating. The body must have been there for a while because it was partly decomposed.

We lifted the body of a factory worker out of the hole. His face was rotting, and his eyes stared blankly at us. We loaded him on one of the lorries and a considerate soldier covered the corpse with some jute from the broken sugar bags. It did not really affect me any more. I saw death every day.

After finishing our work-day we marched back to camp. It was unbelievable how powerful the bombing raids were. Whole blocks of buildings were totally in ruins.

One of the bombs hit a bunker that we sometimes used. An officer interrupted our march and ordered us to help the rescuers. The fire brigade had extinguished the flames but the task of removing the bodies was still in progress. It was a direct hit that had killed all the occupants. I helped remove bodies, some of them young, nice looking female secretaries from the adjoining offices. The bodies were not damaged, they looked almost alive.

I especially recall one beautiful blonde, with long, georgeous hair. She could not have been more then 21. She was laying on a half-collapsed sofa. Dressed in a dark blue, two piece suit, she looked so attractive. The body was totally intact, almost alive. She wore a thin, white blouse and high heeled shoes. Her skirts were blown upwards and her small pinkish panties, with the girdle and the four elastic straps to hold up the stockings, were all exposed.

I had never seen a naked young lady so my shock was a double one. We pulled her out and her stockings, with the dark seams on the back were perfectly in line. Her eyes were closed and she looked as if she were asleep. Her bra, showing through the dusty and half open blouse was different from what I had imagined. Then we found another woman. She was a little older. Her left leg was crushed under a beam from the collapsed ceiling. She had a terrible expression frozen on her face.

What a horrible way to die.

The new American bombs were of such a magnitude that the human body, exposed to such an explosion, would crush inside.

There were more of the office people. We dug and we dug.

Then I recalled the times when the Germans, without any reason, had killed many Polish people. They called it reprisals.

What goes around, comes around. Now, they were the victims of their own war.

The American bombs were getting bigger and stronger. Rumors circulated that they were experimenting with a powerful weapon that could destroy half of Germany in one fell swoop.

Late that evening we were dismissed. Dead tired, we staggered to the camp, washed and ate our meager meal of soup and bread and fell exhausted into bed.

Another day passed and I was still alive. Lying in bed I thought about the long gone days when my Mother would take me to the opera to enjoy Lehar's and Strauss' operettas.

Memorizing the songs I hoped I might one day become a famous tenor. Thoughts of becoming a doctor, a film producer, a movie star or an aeronautic engineer had also been my dreams. I did not realize then that art would become part of my life's work.

Chapter 20

VOAYAGE TO HELSINKI

The German policy of moving labourers away from their own countries to foreign territory had merit. The language and lack of contacts would limit the joining of underground activities. Thus the reason of my being sent to Finland.

Under the cover of night, our group was transported from Szczecin to Gdansk in a column of old army trucks. In the morning sunshine we formed a marching unit and proceeded to the harbour passing through the big iron gates, fortified with bags of sand and machine gun nests.

The fresh sea breeze brought with it the typical smells of the sea: salt water and fish. Our departure was not immediate so we had time to relax and look around.

We sat on the pavement clutching to our belongings in a side bag or a rolled bundle. Once again, I had a blanket hanging over one shoulder and small side bag over the other, containing my Polish ID card, once issued by the Underground. I was still the fictitious Marian Chmielowicz. My personal guard, the German Wehrmacht soldier, a fat, older man named Rosenkopf, was still accompanying me.

The harbour was very busy and I watched the ships. They were mostly old merchant boats. If there were any war ships they were well camouflaged. High ranking officers were saying goodbye to friends, people seemed to rush all over the place for no obvious purpose. Shabby looking war prisoners (we looked not much better) worked filling up bomb holes and repairing some twisted cranes. I was happy that there was no air raid right at that moment and said so to my friends.

"Yes, we would not stand much chance of surviving here. Not too many places to hide except the sea," one of them answered.

I watched a group of Russian prisoners with a Wehrmacht guard repair a hole in the pavement, placing the last round cobblestones in the surface of the pier. They were slow and the two soldiers guarding them also looked sleepy.

"Get up and form the column!" came a clear command to our group. We marched over a gangplank and boarded an old, rusty ship named the

"Nordfolk." It looked like it had been built at least 40 years earlier. It may have been confiscated from the Norwegian merchant marine.

Once on board, we were given our instructions. In the centre of the ship deck was a wooden corral-like fence. It consisted of two rows of rough planks held together by fence poles. We were told that the ship would carry German troops and we were to stay inside the fence while on deck. We were warned that anyone crossing it would be shot.

Below deck there were several levels, all rusty, unpainted and dark. The few bare light bulbs did not brighten much the corridors. The walls, floors and ceilings were constructed of thick, unpainted metal sheets. Any time something was dropped or banged, the loud sound echoed throughout the ship. In the partial darkness I could see the endless rows of bunkbeds made with rough planks. There was a good supply of reasonably fresh straw on the platforms. I could smell and see that before the bunkbeds were installed, the horses had been transported in this area. Their droppings were still there filling the air with an unpleasant smell. We could move freely, but there were many doors with clear signs; "NUR FUR DEUTSCHE" and "ZUTRITT VERBOTEN", [Only for Germans and No Access]. On every level there was a "Dolmetscher" [Interpreter] who explained the rules and regulations. He yelled in a loud voice in Polish, Ukrainian, Croatian, Serbian, French and Italian.

"U-Boot Alarm" was a special signal blown by the ship's main stack announcing attacking submarines. We were ordered to the deck but to stay within our barriers. When the "Flugzeug Alarm" [Air attack] sounded we were ordered to go to the bottom of the ship to avoid the bombs from the attacking planes. There was a third important alarm: "Abandon the ship," but we knew bloody well that there were no lifeboats for the labourers. So, we did not pay very much attention to that particular alarm.

The ship's management decided to give us special treatment. They had several huge wooden barrels of salted butter which began to spoil. They let us open one and help ourselves to all the butter we could eat. For a change, there was an almost sufficient quantity of bread available. It was black and full of wood shavings but it tasted reasonably fresh. We were hungry. Our stomachs were not used to all that butter. Consequently, the line-ups for the few toilets were long.

I sat there watching all this and remembering one day, a long time ago, when my brother Roman had a party with some friends. They roasted a chicken in a new, "modern" way, which called for packing the chicken in semisoft clay, feathers and all. It was put on a bonfire and when ready, the feathers would fall off stuck to the fried clay. The chicken was not cooked well enough and they all got sick.

On the ship, having had some experience with German food, I ate with caution. I took my portion of bread and some butter to the deck. I sat with a couple of friends enjoying the food and the fresh air. A Jewish boy named Stan was one of my friends. I did not know how he had escaped German imprisonment and execution. He was a young man, tall and handsome. He had an excellent memory, spoke fluent German and could recite from his memory long Polish poems by Adam Mickiewicz and other poets. In the darkness of the long nights, he would often entertain us with fantasy stories.

Watching the loading we enjoyed our sandwiches. The traffic connected with the departure of the three merchant ship convoy was fascinating. The harbour activity was feverish. Ship cranes lifted vehicles, small cannons and stacks of ammunition packaged in wooden crates on board. There was a constant flow of motorcycles with sidecars. Helmet-clad drivers picked up and delivered papers and parcels. They carried machine guns on their backs. A big lorry at the next ship was unloading metal cans full of milk. One of the cans somehow slipped out of the loading net and made a big splash in the middle of the loading dock. The place was full of heel-clicks and the "Heil Hitler" salutes. That still looked funny to us. The scene was theatrical and much of the action appeared absurd. We exchanged a few quiet laughs as we watched the performances.

For centuries, Gdansk, sitting quietly on the shores of the Baltic Sea between Poland and East Prussia, flourished. Both the Germans and the Poles had equal access to the city and its harbours. For centuries, it had also been a point of dispute between the two nations. In the distance, we could see the City of Gdansk. Up to 1939, it was a Free Port, a city which, after the First World War and through the Versaille Pact did not actually belong to Poland or to Germany.

Finally, the whistles blew and the thick steel ropes were disconnected and winched onboard, commands rang in the air. Some people waved, but most stood watching sullenly. We had a great location, not at the railing of the ship, but high enough that we could see and follow what was happening.

The majority of the troops on our ship were green uniformed Wehrmacht, but there were also some in black uniforms - the Gestapo. They had absolutely nothing to do with us, we were totally ignored and that was fine with us. As a work-brigade or whatever the Germans called us, we were an uninteresting bunch of labourers from many countries, people of many backgrounds and cultures only needed for our muscles.

The Poles stuck together as did the majority of the other nationalities. Each had their own interpreters, their own ways to solve problems and their own judgment system. As a group of people, isolated from governing and justice systems, we had to create a system for ourselves, so that order could be maintained. The official language was, of course, German. That stayed the same but the nationalities and home languages among all these workers were different.

The metal ship was vibrating, but the engines had a rhythmical hum which was reassuring. The ships slowly started to move out, one after another; we were on our way. It was my very first trip on an high sea going ship, and I was excited despite the circumstances. The pier seem to retreat backward and became smaller and smaller. The sun was shining, it was a perfect day ahead of us. In a little while the land disappeared from sight. I could feel the swell of the sea, there were no waves but the boat was rolling gently. Some guys got seasick so I went below deck. There, under the dim light of a hanging bulb we played cards.

After a while I climbed back up to the deck. After the darkness below, my eyes hurt in the bright light of a gorgeous afternoon. I looked around and noticed two cannons, fore and aft, with quadruple barrels sticking up. Aha, I thought, even the camouflaged merchant ships carry some armament. There were no crews manning them. I wondered how often they were used.

The convoy had stretched out. The two other ships were ahead of us and to the side. We were in the middle and a few miles behind. We were making good time judging from the brisk wake behind the ships. I was looking at the enormous body of water surrounding us and my thoughts went back in time again.

I learned to swim during that vacation. On the outskirts of the village, toward the big "puszcza" [forest], were some fields where the villagers were hand-digging deep rectangular holes taking out "torf" [peat moss], *the centuries old layers of entangled roots. These were cut into brick size cubes and stacked up. When dried, they became excellent fuel for the stoves. The dugouts, six foot by twenty foot, were filled up with swampy ground water. These were mysterious pools, black as an ink well, and there were lots of stories about people drowning in them. Exciting! They were deep enough for us children and so we learned how to swim. We could just jump in and be on the other side by the impact alone.*

Now back on the convoy to Helsinki, a chill came over me on the ships' deck as the sun set. None of us had warm clothes, we did not stay long on the deck. Before going below, I took a last long look at the beautiful horizon thinking that somewhere out there was Sweden and freedom. The convoy stretched out. It was a lonely view. What would the future bring to me?

We went below deck and got ready for our "bunker-soup". The meal, however, was a surprise. We were given fried fish and potatoes as well as soup. We wondered if it were a special day or if the ships were equipped with food for the troops and we were getting better leftovers.

Little by little, guys started to crawl up into the continuous bunkbeds. I followed the others, amassing a nest of straw around my body. I unrolled my blanket and used the side bag as a pillow. The place was actually quite warm. The single electric bulb, hanging from the ceiling, swayed slowly back and forth.

The next morning was bright and full of sunshine. After our breakfast, Stan told a rough war joke. With slightly subdued voice he started:

"Stalin visited Hitler and was shown all the modernization and improvements in the Great Third Reich. After getting back home to Moscow, he invited Hitler to visit him. After a big dinner with lots of vodka and plenty of Russian caviar, Hitler had to go to the bathroom.

Here Stalin had a new invention ready! A man stood underneath on a platform equipped with a long handled broom with the end wrapped in toilet paper. When Hitler finished, he wiped his bottom. However Hitler was jealous and wanted to find out what kind of invention it was. So he bent down to take a look and the man thinking it was an 'encore', wiped him again."

Booom.....booooom......booooooom......, the long signal announcing a U-Boat attack almost stopped him from finishing the story.

Were we sinking or had we been torpedoed? We did not want to be below if a big, torpedo came through the side walls. We grabbed our

belongings and climbed to the deck running as fast as possible. Approaching the opening to our "corral," I heard lots of explosions and the roar of engines. In the general commotion, I could see several Germans shooting up in the air, but the bright sunlight was blinding me and I fell face down. The explosions were very, very loud.

Peeking over the edge of my side bag which was under my head I could see a green clad person lying beside me. It was a young, German officer, he could not be older than me, lying on "his" side of the fence. His face was buried in one arm and the other was stretched up pointing and emptying a black Luger pistol into the sky. A German Luger is a heavy 9 mm pistol which makes lots of noise.

Nobody was shooting at me, so I sat up to get a better look around. Two double fuselage P-38 Lightning planes carrying the British insignia were dive-bombing our convoy. All flacks, the four barrel anti-aircraft cannons from the three ships, were shooting rapidly.

The water was full of shrapnel induced foam. One of the fast moving planes made a big circle around the convoy while the other was diving

from the rear aiming at the lead boat in front of us. She was diving so low that was almost touching the wave tops. Our front flack was silent for a moment while the ammunition belt was changed but the rear one was shooting steadily.

Suddenly, there was a direct hit on the starboard companion ship and their rear cannon and ammunition and the people operating them flew through the air in a ball of fire. The Germans had hit their own ship: they had aimed too low following the fast moving plane. The P-38's made another quick approach and by that time the deck was full of green and black uniformed Germans and every one of them was emptying his weapon. The air was practically gray with bullets. It was a spectacular sight but it was a useless exercise.

The planes went quickly through their maneuvers and disappeared in the distance. Nobody was paying any attention to us as we quietly applauded the little victory of the British divebombers. The Germans had casualties, they did not. The fire following the explosions on the neighboring ship was quickly extinguished and everything returned to normal.

"Boy, the Krauts got excited and forgot what they were aiming at," said Stan. "I am glad it wasn't at our ship. I bet there was lots of shrapnel debris flying around from that explosion."

We had another unusually good meal that evening, played some cards and observed the lights from the coast of Sweden which made us again to dream about an escape.

I woke up the next morning at daybreak. Something was wrong, we were not moving. I went to the deck to see what had happened. We were in a dense fog with the visibility limited to no more than ten metres. Every minute or so, the ship's main stack was producing a sad wailing sound. It was what woke me up. The sound echoed back and once in a while the fog horns of the two other ships could be heard. The engines had stopped and the ship was still except for the gentle motion of the sea.

The thought of escape struck me. The shores of Sweden, a neutral country, should be close by. The Baltic was not very wide where we were. The idea really excited me. There was no one around and the rubber dinghies were just few a feet away, ready, with a turn of a handle, to slide into the sea. I thought I could let one go when the fog-horn sounded, no one would hear the splash.

I was about to bend down to cross under the wood fence when ahead of me appeared the silhouette of a German officer, and momentarily another one. They were talking in subdued voices and I knew they would see and hear me in the extremely quiet morning which was broken only by the occasional fog siren. I would have been a sitting duck. My plan became impossible.

The fog started to disperse and we could distinguish the shapes of the other ships just a few kilometers to the side. The engines came to life and we began to move again. The fog was almost gone and a beautiful, bright day started to take shape all around us.

In the evening of the third day we arrived at the port of Helsinki. Approaching the inlet, we enjoyed the charm of the Finnish shoreline. It consisted of hundreds of low, smooth polished rocks which, in the setting sun, looked like a bunch of whales having a family reunion. The rocks were very smooth, shiny and red. "This area must have a lot of iron ore," I thought to myself.

The ship moved slowly into the harbour. Commands and whistles rang in the air, lines were tossed and received, and small towing boats guided us. Helsinki was a busy port and with the arrival of these three big ships became even busier.

Gangplanks were raised, the German troops marched ashore and then it was our turn.

"Schnell...schnell...Menscheskind, vergiss deine Sachen nicht". [Hurry up, you dummies, don't forget your belongings], the guards urged us on.

On the dock we were lined up and counted and as the sky darkened, we were marched to our destination for the night. After a few hundred metres we approached some elegant fenced villas. Our group was separated from the others and went through some beautiful gardens, past a large, ornamental, wrought iron gate to the main entrance of a castle-like white villa with tall, white pillars on both sides of the enormous, carved door. I could not believe my eyes. We entered an imposing, well kept mansion, full of large, stately rooms, all of which had polished, hand-laid hardwood floors. Not a single carpet was seen anywhere or a piece of furniture. The place was empty.

"Make yourselves at home," said the OT guard. None of them carried any weapons now, but they wore brown OT uniforms with swastikas on the sleeves. Many of them were Austrians who hated Hitler. So instead of being sent to the frontline, they were assigned this work brigade. We were in a way, very lucky.

We walked through all the glorious rooms and an enormous kitchen. Everything was perfect. It actually looked like a small castle. We were free to move as we wished. Nobody asked any questions.

I wandered out to the terraces at the the property's back. Large, beautifully designed and well cared for gardens could be seen from here. With just a glimmer of light in clouds where the sun had set, I was about to turn around to go in and find myself good floor space where I could sleep, when something caught my eye. There was distinct undulating movement all over the gardens. What could it be, moving here and there all over the place?

I strained my eyes and could see the place was infested with large rats which were running, jumping and sitting everywhere. There were literally thousands of them. Like a small wave they moved in the now dark landscape. Where did they come from? Were they harmful?

As I went to sleep, my thoughts turned toward home, wondering how my Mother was, what had happened to friends and how the "Ponury's" partisans were surviving, and I pondered the insanity of the Germans. Hours ago, we were in a wooden corral on the Baltic Sea and now in a stylish, luxurious villa.

Chapter 21

SHOT FOR SARDINES

The next morning we began our journey to the north of Finland. We were marched to the railroad station. The Finnish Railroad System had the traditional red painted boxcars to transport goods or cattle. The cars were shorter than the European version, which caused them to bump noisely while in motion. The main troop transport train had several such boxcars attached to its end. We were herded into these small cars. Here we were between 20 or 25 men in each straw filled car. It was almost totally dark when the doors were slammed shut.

After a long whistle, the train began to move and immediately I heard the irritating sound of the short car trying to negotiate the old, outdated tracks with a loud: "Pa-dat...pa-dat...pa-dat..." We had to get used to that sound. The trip, we were told, would take seven days.

We still had Rosenkopf with us guarding all our movements.

"No running away," threatened Herr Rosenkopf looking at me with a smile, "or I shoot." We sat down in the straw and he opened up a small wrapped rag bundle and produced a piece of square, black bread "Ferpflegungs Brot" and a sausage and began to eat. I reached into my small side bag and found some hard crackers. Stan, my Jewish friend, was lying beside me and munching on something while the wheels of the train sang their monotone "Pa-dat...pa-dat....pa-dat...."

In the late afternoon the train halted. The watchman opened the sliding door and we saw thick forest on each side of the track. Commands were shouted and we all jumped off the high embankment. Saws and axes were produced and we were marched into the woods.

"Schnell, schnell.." [hurry!] shouted the Germans as we were made to compete with the approaching darkness. It was our task to cut a number of one metre long logs for the locomotive.

After the fires and burning smells in Gdansk and Szczecin in northern Poland, the sweet forest air filled my lungs and gave me enormous pleasure. I was relieved that the Germans had arrested me on the streets of Warszawa during a regular street "Lapanka." Labour camp seemed to have saved my life without knowing it. Many things had happened to me

since that arrest but I was still alive, and the possibility of my survival looked brighter and better day by day.

Our job completed, the train got underway again. At midnight, we stopped at a large station where we were allowed to walk on the platform and stretch our legs. We were given soup with some meat and dark bread. The food made its way to our empty stomachs very quickly. An hour later we were ordered back to the train and settled in for the night as we again rolled northward. "Pat - dat...pat - dat...pat - dat...."

I heard some voices and saw some movement during the night. Somebody was asking me if I wanted something and I said "No." I was not awake enough to find out what it was. Soldier Rosenkopf was peacefully snoring beside me, his gun lying in the straw beside him. The morning light was starting to seep through the cracks of the car when somebody shook my shoulder. The train was rhythmically saying "Pa - dat...pa - dat... pa - dat" and watchman Rosenkopf was still sleeping. One of the guys put his fingers over his lips in a motion indicating not to wake the German.

"Here, take some sardines, we just climbed over to the supply car and stole them. They are good."

I was afraid to.

"No, thanks, I am not hungry and I don't like sardines," I lied to him. I loved sardines and would have liked to eat some, but something told me to refuse. The fellow went to the others and I fell asleep again.

In the morning the train came to a stop at a large station.

"Raus, Raus!", shouted the Germans. "Alle Leute raus." [everybody out]. Take all your belongings with you.

Why, I wondered, we were not in North Finland yet. We were standing on a big square with a lot of people. They marched us to one side and commanded us to form a row. Suddenly some Politzei and Schutzpolitzei began to roughly search us, one by one. The people who had sardine boxes were put to one side. I realized then that the Germans found out somebody had broken into the supply car and they were looking for the culprits. The guys with the sardines were lined up by some trees on one side of the big square. The Germans brought out a machine gun, erected it on a tripod and before we knew they cut down offenders with ugly bursts of heavy machine gun fire.

The civilian population quickly deserted the square in utter horror. All shaking, I thanked the Almighty God that I had not given in to the temptation to put some of the sardines into my backpack.

I felt I had used up yet another life.

The blood covered bodies of our friends were left there in the square for everybody to see.

We were standing on that plattform left to ourselves. In order to escape this horror, I again drifted mentally back in time.

"Tatus" liked to hunt. He took us on the village lake in an old boat, hand chiseled from a tree-trunk. The ducks were not afraid and let us get quite close. Father had an antique, double barrelled 16 gauge shotgun. I always covered my ears when he was about to pull the trigger. I did not like the sight of bloody carcasses fished out of the water but my mother cooked unbelievably tasty dishes using these wild ducks. Just to forget the horrible situation I continued to remember that in those days we also went to the forest to pick up a variety of wild mushrooms which were white but with pinkish blades underneath. When fried in fresh butter, they were aromatic and tasted delicious.

But food was the wrong memory. It had just cost lives and I was jarred back to the present.

We were back here in the middle of north Finland and expected to eat breakfast. Every face looked strained because of what we had just witnessed. We were sent back to the boxcars and the train started to roll again.

We cut lots of the Finnish timber on our week long journey. When we stopped in some larger towns, I thought of making another escape attempt. I did not know the language, which is the most difficult one among the Scandinavian, and knew that if I came across an informer or a Nazi (Finland had some of them too) my life would come to an end. The Germans would not hesitate to shoot an escapee since after all they had killed many for a lousy box of sardines.

Chapter 22

KOLOSJOKI

Shaken by the events of the boxcar ride from Helsinki, we finally arrived north of the Polar Circle. It was a little town named Kolosjoki. As usual, we were marched to our destination, this time barracks in a picturesque, wooded area. These were large, one room, well built huts. Bunks occupied one side and a large wood burning stove stood in the center of the other. A few benches and a couple of rough tables completed the furnishings. There were windows on the front side only. Deep forests of spruce and pine trees covered the entire area with a few foot paths leading into them.

The Germans had more comfortable huts and their own kitchen. Very few of the OT men carried weapons. I recall one, a kindly looking guy, who would whinny like a horse. The story had it that he became so angry with the authorities who forcibly removed him from his home in Austria that he went kind of crazy. He kept up the act for the rest of the war.

The commandant of the camp was extremely afraid of criticism from his bosses and the possibility of a transfer to the Eastern front. Most of the Germans feared this immensely. The rumor in the camp was that the commandant had been a professor at one of the Austrian universities, a certified engineer, specialist in concrete construction.

The whole camp was surrounded with a loosely structured fence. There was a guard at the gate, but he never stopped anybody and the gate was never closed. We were not prisoners of war but were treated like slave laborers.

Everyone was assigned to various barracks. To our horror, we discovered that these accommodations were infested with bedbugs. They were dark brown creatures which, after sucking your blood were fat and reddish the size of a hearing aid battery. They came out at night and managed to find their way to warm bodies.

To prevent this I tried every trick I knew. Electricity was turned off at night so we had candles. I knew that the bedbugs hated the frozen, uninsulated floor so I pulled a narrow, wooden bench to the middle of the room and put my bedding on it. My bed clothes consisted of a woolen blanket, a raincoat and my side bag as a pillow. But I could not outsmart them. I woke up in the middle of the night, uncomfortable and scratching myself to the accompaniment of all the snoring guys in the bunk beds. I lit a candle in order to find out what was causing me to itch all over. What confronted my half open eyes was a long column of bedbugs walking across the dark ceiling stopping exactly over my position and dropping one by one onto my make-up bed.

Fortunately, this acute problem was brought to the attention of the camp officers. One morning a few more OT men came in to wake us up.

"Get up fast, you good for nothing sonofabitches, and take all your clothing with you!" shouted the soldiers. "You are going to be desinfected, and any clothes left behind here will be burned."

Within a few minutes we formed a marching column and were directed to a nearby building. It was used that day to desinfect people and their clothes but otherwise functioned as a bakery. A few Germans were there as well. We undressed and put our clothes on a big metal sheet that was slid into a baker's stove. Temporary pipes had been strung along one wall of the large room and we were all told to take a shower. Strong soap, which smelled dreadful and stung our eyes was distributed along with large rice brushes, normally used to scrub the floors.

"This is paradise, no work today," said one of my friends. One thing for sure. We felt the Germans would not disinfect people they were going to shoot. That was an unspoken belief. Every day we expected that something unusual might happen and we would be executed.

One of the Germans laughed. He was a big, red haired man, waving his hairy arms in the cold shower.

"Old Wolfgang will have to get us some new clothes. They kept them in the oven too long and they all burned." He found that very amusing.

We felt clean after the mutual scrubbing and there was nothing biting us any more. Every thing smelled fresh and clean. The biggest surprise was when we got back to the barracks, and found the floors and the walls dusted with a nasty-smelling white chemical powder.

Camp routine was established. At 5:00 a.m. we would be awaken abruptly. We had half an hour to get water, heat it on the stove, wash and dress for the line up. We were counted and assigned to our different jobs.

I was young and healthy, so I was put on a nickel strip mining crew. We were driven in cattle trucks to a mine just a few kilometres away. Our crew worked all day long, with half an hour at noon to eat the dreadful "bunker soup". This lunch was being brought to us by the kitchen delivery staff. The German cooks in Finland used the same recipe as the cooks in Szczecin: boiled water with a slight vegetable taste and lots of salt. In the liquid floated pieces of questionable origin. With this we had two pieces of the black bread.

The labourers developed a sharing system for the food to avoid arguments. Whatever had arrived in bulk to be shared, whether it was a block of margarine, (which we received twice a week) or the daily bread, we organized ourselves in fours. One would do the dividing and the others had the first choice. This way, there were no complaints. We were always hungry, tired and cold, so small issues could develop into major fights.

I listened to the watchman shouting at one of the other crews: "Schnell...schnell...faule Leute, die anderen sind schon fertig." [Hurry up, you lazy people, the others have already finished]. I kept enjoying my couple of minutes rest before the next row of mining carts arrived. They were standing ready on a little sidetrack, waiting.

One day, hunger made us desperate. Some of the guys found a dog, slit its throat, skinned the carcass behind the barracks, and made a stew in a big old kettle on the stove. Some onions and potatoes, probably taken from the German kitchen, were added. The aroma of home cooking filled our barracks. I do not recall the particular taste but I am sure it was delicious. We had our own utensils, zinc mugs and bowls, so everybody got a bowlful and then it remained a barrack No. 7's secret.

Another time, as part of a three man partnership, we did some trading. I had made a couple of pencil portraits of some of the OT officers. Even some of the Germans did not get enough sugar and we had been saving our rations for weeks. With my sketches and some sugar to exchange we got a couple of extra loaves of bread. The Germans baked their own bread, supplying the entire camp. A loaf of bread was the size of two bricks, small, heavy and rectangular.

That evening the three of us made bread soup in a big kettle, with lots of water, the two loaves and some sugar. In the late hours, by the light of a single candle, we filled our bellies with the food and were envied by the others. We could not but share it with our equally hungry bunk mates.

A narrow gage mining train was lined up in front of us. "Arbeiten, arbeiten, Menscheskind" [Work, work, you dummies] said the watchman walking back and forth on a little higher plateau with his Mauser rifle hanging over his shoulder. And we shovelled the rocks of heavy metal, covered with thick dust, to the mining carts, which were banged-up here and there but served their purpose well. The grey dust was everywhere, in our mouths and noses, in our hair and eyes, and, of course, in all of our clothes. We brushed and brushed but it did not help at all.

Our mining cart was full so we sat down. I took a piece of the rock in my hand and with a small pocket knife began to scrape it. After only a couple of strokes it became shiny like chrome. No wonder the Germans put such a high priority on this area. The nickel ore here had over 73% pure metal in it, an important resource in the war. With all that concentrated, almost pure nickel the Russians were after it too. Nickel mining was hard work. To increase production, the Germans would choose a team of very strong men and then force the other teams to work just as fast. The metal cars were pushed in front of us and we were urged to to fill them up quickly so the locomotive could pull the train away. The few minutes it took to empty them was our only short break before we had to start again. We worked ten hours a day. We were totally exhausted and becoming weak. Some of the men collapsed and were taken away.

One morning, in the fall, we lined up for the usual head count. The commandant asked us:

"Wir brauchen Elektriker." [We need electricians]. It did not occur to me right away, but somewhere in the back of my mind and through the numbness of my exhausted body, something started to ring a bell!

I stepped forward. "Ich bin ein," [I am a one] I tried to say loudly and clearly but the words got stuck in my throat.

"Was hast du gesagt?" [What did you say?] asked the commandant.

I repeated a little louder: "Ich bin ein Elektriker".

"Give me your Ausweis".

I fumbled with my sore hands under my jacket and shirts and produced the worn out, little book. He waved to me to bring it to him. I staggered forward and handed it over. He looked through it carefully. I started to shake fearing he would recognize the faked ID.

"Ah, ja, du bist ein Elektriker." [Yes-you are an electrician].

The big violet stamp with a signature clearly stated that I was an electrician. It was put there by the Germans when I was caught in Warszawa and asked my profession. The stamp was genuine.

I was told to go back to the barrack and take off the heavy overalls. I was ordered to present myself to hut No. 22 and ask for a certain Herr Haberbeyer, but not before 8 a.m.

It was only 6:15.

Exhausted, I went back to the empty barrack. I could not believe my luck. There was some water left on the hot stove so I washed myself a little better.

At 8 sharp I was in front of barracks No. 22 asking for Herr Haberbeyer. Haberbeyer was a heavy built, friendly Austrian who enjoyed life and did not seem to hurry if it was not necessary. He looked me over and asked me a few questions in broken Polish. We walked to the German parking lot, got in a small truck and drove away. I was approved. Being driven to work in a private German vehicle was an unbelievable luxury.

The Finish roads in the far north were not very good, constructed only of gravel and sand with lots of ungraded curves. We arrived at a little turn around at end of the road. There was no road beyond that point only rocks and subarctic trees with lots of black moss. The sun was shining and birds were singing. How beautiful the world could be!

We walked a little distance and came to a more open area. There were groups of Russian and Ukrainian prisoners, digging holes, cutting trees and moving rocks. They had Wehrmacht watchmen guarding them.

"Come over here, Marian," Herr Haberbyer said in his deep voice, "I have the first job for you."

He was standing with a higher ranking German officer holding some large blueprints and discussing them.

"Here, my little one, put these on and climb that pole," he pointed at one debarked tree. The Russian prisoners had a short time ago stuck the pole in a newly dug hole and put some large stones around.

I sat down and looked. In front of me I had two large, curved metal hooks with pieces of flat iron welded to them at one end. There were some ropes attached to it.

"Go ahead," said Herr Haberbeyer and walked away to the waiting officer. My mind raced. I had never seen such contraptions before. I quickly realized that they must be used for climbing the poles. I started to put them on. Mr. Haberbeyer barked "Heil Hitler" to the officer who walked away to the parking lot. Soon he came over and I stood up.

"Ha...ha...ha...hah," boomed Herr Haberbeyer with his stomach shaking up and down, "you cannot climb a pole like that."

"Are you really an electrician? You want me to send you back?" He added in a lower voice.

"If I do, you will not survive." He became serious, stopped laughing and said,

"Switch them around, you have the right one on your left foot - you Dummkopf." I was thankful that they were short of properly trained helpers and that Haberbeyer was a good man.

For the first time in my life I climbed up a pole. The pole, the last in a line of many, was heavier than the others designed to resist the weight of the entire electrical conduit. In the meantime, the group of the Russian prisoners were setting up many more, one after another, stretching away in the direction from which we had come.

Herr Haberbeyer, was guiding me step by step. Climbing a power pole was not complicated, but I was glad that for my first lesson, I had such a good and friendly teacher.

"No, not like that, put your weight on your heel so the hooks bite into the wood... Jawohl, that's better. Oh, you're learning quickly."

I was climbing higher and higher. I liked the feel of the belt around my waist and the pole. With each step I took I lifted the belt, and before I knew it, I was at the top.

"Don't go so high that your belt flips over the top. If you do, you're dead just like that," and he ran his flat hand across his throat. As he was saying this, the officer came back and called him, "Haberbeyer, Haberbeyer, come here for a moment!", he shouted waving at my new boss and getting him over to explain something. As their discussion continued, I had time to look around.

How free one felt at the top of the world. The sun was shining and I had a new career. I glanced around. The two were bending down now, pointing at the blueprints spread on the ground and discussing something with great intensity.

Even if I had wanted to I could not have heard anything because of constant ringing in my ears. My lungs hurt a little when I took a deep breath, possibly from all the dust from the nickel mine.

The other day one of the guys suggested, when I told him about my pain, that I should pierce my finger and add a drop of blood to my sputum and show it to the Germans. That was what he was planning to do in order, he hoped, to be sent back home. They were afraid of people with the tuberculosis which the blood indicated.

I looked the other way, and saw some trees and bushes and the same type of pink rocks all around. Looking further, I was suddenly stunned to see, only a few hundred meters away, two Russian soldiers in full uniforms and with guns over their shoulders. I could even distinguish their red stars on their fur hats. Then I saw a heavy machine gun pointing straight at me. They must have been looking at me for quite a while, because seeing my surprise they waved at me and seemingly SMILED.

Haberbeyer was back. The other fellow was gone. I was shaken and had a hard time relaying what I had seen.

"Meister Haberbeyer, I see Russian soldiers; their guns are pointed at me," I stammered. "What is happening here?"

He only laughed; his big stomach dancing up and down again.

"You make me feel so good with your jokes, you little polisher Knabe. Don't you know that we are at the border? There, over that hill, is Russia."

He threw a string attached to a little stone and asked me to pull up the ends of two wires, which I did. He then guided me step by step. I attached them to the pole and secured them. I was breathing easier but still keeping an eye on the soldiers. Slowly, I calmed down.

The days went by. We were moving west with the power transmission line, away from the Russian border. Day by day it grew in length.

Chapter 23

SOMEWHERE IN NORTHERN FINLAND 1944
THE RUSSIAN INVASION
ESCAPE TO NORWAY

After a few weeks, the job was completed and we had reached the power switch house. Somebody else would now continue to build the lines. I had no idea where these lines were going. I had the impression that the Germans were thinking about developing more nickel mines and industries that required electric power.

I got a job installing light switches, ceiling lamp sockets and other electric work in the barracks and houses around us. It was an easy life. I put small messages in the cavities, before screwing the plates back on. The messages usually read: "Polish hands have built this outlet."

The Russian and Ukrainian prisoners were sent to help with the nickel mining. One day, one of the Russian prisoners, wearing nice mountain boots, suggested in broken Polish that he would like to make a trade with me. He chose me because I was intently looking at his attractive boots. We traded my new but ugly work boots for his nice mountain boots.

Within one week the soles of my "new" boots started to come off. They were old and rotten right through. I learned another valuable lesson about treachery. I never saw the man again. Instead, often at night we heard the Russian prisoners sing in the barracks their melancholic military songs praising Stalin and a few top Soviet commanders, Voroshilov, Timoshenko and others. Despite all suffernigs in Russia and here in the Nazi labour camps, they still venerated their Great Butcher.

Through the dark northern winter, life went on. I was still alive and my lungs were getting better. Everyday, I learned something new in the electrical field. Luckilly for me, I learned how to repare fuses and to run small extension lines. But it did not last forever.

One morning, from the northern direction of Petsamo, we heard a distant canon, the explosions of heavy artillery fire and machine guns.

THE RUSSIANS HAD ATTACKED !

We had five minutes to pack. The labour force was loaded in trucks and sent on the only, narrow, winding mountain road away from the front line. No more electrician job, we were again all together. The convoy drove most of the morning until we stopped at an abandoned, empty camp. We were ordered to clean the place immediately. The barbed wire fence was in place but dilapidated wood buildings needed much repair. The front line moved so fast that we were, almost immediately, transported further south.

I befriended a very interesting young fellow, an Austrian. He had been forced to join the German submarine service and had somehow managed to escape and hide in our labour force. He was also a trained pilot.

In the darkness of the night he taught us how to start and take off in a Junkers-87 aircraft. We spent night after night studying the sequences until we knew them thoroughly. His dream was to steal a plane and fly over to Sweden which was only few kilometers away. As Sweden remained neutral and untouched by the Germans during the Second World War, it was a dream destination for all of us. Each night, a couple of us involved in the conspiracy repeated the location of all the buttons and levers, all the sequences of the movements and all the possible dangers to avoid. How exciting it was! This was dangerous because we were surrounded by dozens of men - maybe informers.

In order to study the adjoining airport I pretended that I had a toothache to be sent to a dentist in a small village next to the camp. I walked there alone on the only road going through the mountain ranges. The Germans were not afraid that any of us would escape. We were in an almost empty foreign country, did not speak the language, and were considered workers rather than prisoners. They even attempted to pay us, in Finland with the German Mark which we could not use there, and later in Norway with the Finnish Krona.

The OT commandant told us on several occasions that he knew that some of us were not simply workers but he also hated the Gestapo, so as long as we behaved, no one would be harmed.

We were thinking flying all the time.

One evening I recalled my first exposure to aeroplanes, long ago, before the war. In public school in Warszawa, a bunch of us went to the small airport and, not being spotted, I climbed into one of the double-winged planes and, having learned the procedure, started its engine. My friends removed the wheel-blocks and my machine began to roll down the grassy runway. I was nearly airborne when the plane's

"shut-off" valve or lack of gas, which I did not know about, cut off the supply of fuel. The plane stopped at the far end of the field, I jumped out and ran to the closest street and took the long way home. The word, however, had spread. Next morning at school. I was a hero. Somehow that story never got to the people who would not have thought me a hero.

Now here, far north, I went to the village to find the dentist. He was a nice man, full of good humor, but not very well equipped.

"Toothache, aha, I do not have much to fix it with. All I can do is to pull it. You want me to pull it, aha?"

In this way I lost a few teeth in the next few weeks.

The airfield was a narrow strip of land with some well camouflaged hangars. The few planes on the ground were the Junkers-87s and the Heinkels, a smaller version of a bomber. I had to walk very close and the couple of guards just smiled at me after recognizing the German OT hat I was wearing with my civilian clothes.

Walking by all these military installations I thought, one day, back in time, about my previous experience in photography and how nice it would have been if I had a camera and could do some spying for the Allies.

Taking pictures with a little box-camera also occupied my time as a child. Converting the bathroom to a darkroom, I learned how to develop them. After a while I got myself a little wooden printing frame with glass and was able to make contact prints on a daylight paper. These prints were sepia coloured and I counted by snapping my fingers for the number of seconds of exposure they needed. Producing films with an old shoe box and a cardboard paper tube was another hobby. It was very easy, with an electric bulb and a long strip of paper made of smaller pieces glued together, imitating a film strip, to draw a picture story and show it to everybody casting it on the wall. We had many "Grand Premiere" opening nights when Mom made some special goodies and my brother and I presented our "movies".

We wrote commercials, like we had seen in American movies. All my life my imagination was of such a nature that I was able, on many occasions, to sweat out advertising ideas with great success. I got carried away. How easy I could drift off target.

Here in the north, back in the barracks, we compared notes, made improvements and started to plan our next move. A couple of days before we were going to execute our plan, the Germans moved us to another location further south where there were neither airfields nor aircrafts.

In the new place, located between high mountains, there were also settlers. Some had already left south and others were preparing to be evacuated.

On the days when we were not busy maintaining the road in front of us, where the German columns constantly moved back and forth, we sometimes sat in abandoned buildings and told stories or discussed the approaching end of the war. We talked about the new situation. We had all been through a great deal, nothing was new anymore. In one of the log-houses we sat on a big pile of potatoes. We were tempted to spread gasoline or coal oil over them to make them unpalatable to the Germans; a kind of sabotage. We abandoned this project, however, as there was no use of it. Where would we go to hide? They would find and finish us faster than anything. In another of the old, half rotten sheds, we found a big room full of thousands of shoes, ladies' and men's. Some of them were quite good, but they were not sorted in pairs.

"I am sure, these are shoes of murdered European Jews," speculated Stan, "they brought them here to Scandinavia to do something with them.

But what?" Nobody knew the answer. We only hoped that the war would leave us alone as its end was in sight.

Fortunately, the Germans needed road cleaning and repair crews, so instead of leaving us for the Russians they dragged us along. Our chances for survival were good as long as they needed us.

On one of our last moves we crossed to Norway, which, after the war, became my new country. For thirteen years I lived there, married there, and in 1950, became a proud citizen.

One light, Arctic night, somewhere in the far north in the middle of nowhere, three of us got ahold of a big, Norwegian rowing boat. We rowed over to visit a farm settlement on the other side of a narrow fjord. The night was quiet and the only sound came from the steady movements of the oars. Above us a beautiful night sky twinkled in colours. We had never seen such a sight in Europe. We sat spellbound. I stopped rowing and we drifted in total quietness. The three of us observed the breathtaking Aurora Borealis flicker high above. We sat in silence for a few minutes, everyone agreed that we could not only see but also hear the

Northern Lights as they emitted a tiny, high-pitched sound. The plankton disturbed by the boat and the oars, lit up in a mysterious, bluish glare. We approached the dim lights of the settlement, smoothly and quietly, even the wind was mute.

Reaching our destination, we tied the boat to the pier and walked up to the buildings. A farmer and his family were very nice, but we had difficulty communicating. None of us spoke Norwegian and none of them spoke Polish or German. They put on the coffee and we had a rare, civilized evening. The lady even went to her "stabbur", a very special, decorated log house serving as a food storage. (Every Norwegian farm has one beside the main house to store grain and supplies. The mice cannot get inside as a stabbur is always built on four steep stones.) She brought some flour and baked us something which tasted delicious. After eating some salty dried mutton, called "fenalor" in Norwegian, we tried to communicate again. We drew sketches on a piece of paper and smiled as we tried to carry on a limited conversation. It was such a pleasant evening.

We rowed back full of glory. Nowhere in the world are starry skies so bright and so magnetic as in the far North. We stopped again in the middle of the fjord and sat still in the boat. It was amazing. We could not tell where the sea ended and the sky began. Millions of stars filled the firmament and were reflected in the calm sea. The tops of the surrounding mountains shone in the moonlight. We were one with nature. It created another world, separate from the war torn one we knew only too well.

Chapter 24

THE ROAD TO FREEDOM

Yet again we were driven from the shooting and bombing behind us. We were heading in the south-westerly direction. We could hear the bombardment of Petsamo in the very northern tip of Finland. The truck convoy came to a halt in front of yet another abandoned camp and we were ordered to clean it out and settle in.

It was around Easter time 1945 and the Germans decided to give us a day off. There was in fact nothing to do unless they created a pointless task. We found some skis and a small group of us went for a ski trip, heading east, of course hoping to cross the border to Sweden. We travelled steadily for an hour. The sun was shining and the weather was perfect. On a ridge of a small mountain we stopped.

Ahead of us was a valley, on the opposite slope, we could see against the white snow, small, dark spots moving back and forth. We stared and stared, nobody had binoculars. Finally we realized what we were seeing. The next mountain top was in Sweden but on the slope, the Germans had placed a pack of dogs to warn them if anyone tried to cross. What we saw were the tails of the dogs. We were astonished; not only was the plan weird but we wondered how the Germans had managed it. Sure enough, by the time we changed direction and headed back, a white clad German patrol intercepted us, asked questions and gave us hell for coming so close to the border.

Snow started to fall and it was exactly like pioneer days. We searched for wood for the stove and repaired a couple of broken windows. There was no one else around except our OT men and a very small contingent of Wehrmacht soldiers to guard us. This did not last long.

"Raus, Raus, alle Menschen!" [All people out!]. Assemble outside on the double!" shouted one of the guards, "leave your belongings behind and come, you will be returning tonight." We lined up in the thickly falling snow, were divided into smaller groups and worked up and down the road keeping it cleared for the German army. It became obvious that they were under pressure from the Russians and retreating.

As we shovelled the accumulating snow and sanded slippery spots, dozens upon dozens of vehicles, artillery and trucks full of soldiers started to pass us going south. The faces of the soldiers and the officers were sullen and depressed. It was at this point in the war that I saw several Germans throw their weapons away. All kinds of goodies went down the slopes, machine guns, pistols and rifles. They were a sad looking bunch who knew they were nearing their defeat. The camp routine was relaxed and our guards became indifferent.

On nice days we would be told to take it easy and go for a walk in the mountains. There was nowhere else to go. One day we went off for a couple of hours between the hills and into the mountains. After climbing for a while and looking around I went behind small bushes to relieve myself. I saw some branches leaning strangely against some rocks. Checking closer, I found to my surprise a few old, rotten boards blocking an entrance to a cave. I called the others and we were able to open the entrance. Inside we found furniture, matches, guns, food supplies and other necessities. It looked more civilian then military so we decided it must have been the local people who had prepared an emergency shelter.

We took a piece of dry lamb because we were hungry. The rest we repacked the way we had found it. We ate the meat on the way back so we would not come under suspicion. When we arrived back at the camp, we found it frantic with activity.

Orders to move out again had been given. We were assembled in front of the barracks when we saw a large, white camouflaged truck coming our way. Every a few minutes the truck stopped and some white-dressed German skiers, operating on both sides of the road, destroyed everything around them. They put dynamite around every telephone and power pole and detonated it, breaking the poles to pieces. At one point they put dynamite under the road where it was narrow and crossed over a brook. We could see them clearly on the slope of a majestic mountain across the valley. The explosion was incredible, pieces of black dirt released by the force flew into the air and the echo boomed between the walls of the valley.

Our transportation arrived, but before we were loaded and started on the way, the grim German commandoes set fire to the barracks. We were lucky not to have been shot or abandoned there. After driving for a few hours, we stopped at a camp which was already occupied by other labour force groups.

The Spring of 1945 had arrived. Rumors about the end of the war were frequent and we saw many signs to support these rumors. The German organization disintegrated. German officers and their battalions were retreating south as quickly as possible. Our own German OT men started to disappear and those of us of other nationalities who had been moved to Norway by the Germans were left with very little supervision. Communication between the German troops had broken down and our greatest danger came from isolated groups of Germans who did not realize they were no longer in control.

A group of us having obtained travel permits in the middle of April, managed to hitch a ride with a mail truck going south. After a few days of travel we arrived in Tromso. We went to the German canteen in the main German encampment in the city. We had dinner and the German female waitresses were very nice and polite until I sat at the piano, and played a few tunes, ending with the Polish national anthem. One of the German Wehrmacht corporals came to me and waving his Schmeisser said:

"Where do you think you are? You shouldn't play that here." He pointed to a big portrait of Adolf Hitler hanging right over the piano. I tried to act innocent but somebody else asked him what was going on, and before we knew it we were on the street, getting away before anything could happen.

We travelled on to Trondheim and planned to go to the same type of place to get food. But it was the eighth of May and it was the day the Germans capitulated in Norway. We took part in the celebration. I found a Norwegian family who gladly took my woolen blanket in return for one loaf of bread and one kilogram of margarine. What a feast we had! That is my most vivid memory of the ending of the war.

We arrived in Oslo and we were placed in Gruneløkka School with hundreds of other displaced persons. Imagine, no guards, no weapons, no danger of losing our lives! Unbelievable! We heard some sporadic gun fire the first couple of days and there were rumors that some units of the German Army did not want to capitulate. But that ended very quickly.

Total peace was declared on May 17, Norway's National Independence Day. Joy was unrestrained. Strangers were hugging strangers, kissing each other and crying.

We were free!

What a superb feeling it was!

End of this book.
The Nine Lives continues in Norway. Now in preparation . . .

A Message to the readers, Fall 1996

You may be of Polish, German or other descent. When you read these pages and recognize any of the episodes described therein - please write to me to add details which I might have forgotten. Please send your letter to the Publisher whose address is given on the back of the title page.

LIST OF ILLUSTRATIONS

*WITHOUT SHEILA SPENCER AND HER
FRIEND BERNICE, DAVID GOBBY
OF CONCORDIA UNIVERSITY AND HIS
FATHER-IN-LAW, MY SON ROBERT AND
UNBELIEVABLE PEOPLE LIKE LANTRY
VAUGHAN OF RED DEER COLLEGE,
KARIN OF ATHABASCA UNIVERSITY AND
ANDREW KOBOS OF EDMONTON, WHO
ALL SPENT COUNTLESS HOURS
GUIDING ME THROUGH THE
INTRICACIES OF THE ENGLISH
LANGUAGE - THIS BOOK WOULD
NEVER SEE THE DAYLIGHT.
THEY ALL DID IT FROM THE SHEER
GOODNESS OF THEIR HEARTS.*

THANKYOU ALL! - THE AUTHOR